AF255208

THE SUN STILL SHINES

The Sun Still Shines

The Legend of a Drunken Pastor

C. Don Jones

RESOURCE *Publications* · Eugene, Oregon

THE SUN STILL SHINES
The Legend of a Drunken Pastor

Resource Publications
An Imprint of Wipf and Stock Publishers
199 W. 8th Ave., Suite 3
Eugene, OR 97401

www.wipfandstock.com

PAPERBACK ISBN: 978-1-6667-6124-5
HARDCOVER ISBN: 978-1-6667-6125-2
EBOOK ISBN: 978-1-6667-6126-9

05/22/23

For all the clergy, spiritual leaders, and lay ministers who suffer in silence. Even when faith and love appear to fail, there is hope.

The legend is generally made by the people of the village, who are sane.
The book is generally written by the one man in the village who is mad.

—G. K. CHESTERTON

Contents

Introduction

I never imagined I would be in a scandal. Instead of the scandal of sexual indiscretion that happens with many pastors, I was discovered drunk by a church member. There are actions we scrupulously avoid committing. Then there are actions we never consider bad. Lastly, there are the actions we hide to keep up appearances.

Addiction among the clergy is one of these hidden secrets. During the question-and-answer part of a talk about my own experience, two points were made by members of the audience who were also members of the clergy. The first point was that there were four members of the clergy in the small audience. The second point was there should have been more.

I know too well how a friend appeared to have the local police parked outside of his neighborhood because of all the times he was arrested for driving under the influence. Eventually he ended his life, by accident or intention, leaving the rest of us to wonder what we could have said or done. Too many pastors, evangelists, and ministers die from substance abuse disorders. Some fell into addiction as part of the opioid crisis. Others of us looked for ways to alleviate our psychic pain.

Why do clergy people fail to ask for help? Is it pride, fear, or the newest excuse that one's own problems are not as bad as those who need our help? Reaching out is the easiest action any of us can take. Unfortunately, we feel vulnerable in risking rejection or ridicule.

This book has two objectives. The first is to encourage anyone—especially those who serve religious communities—to ask for help with their mental health issues, especially addictions. It is not enough to say we bring our addictions and lay them at the feet of Jesus expecting healing. Your colleagues love you and will help.

A few months back an old friend said, "You look better than I have ever seen you." I thanked her and talked about how my doctor said I was doing regarding my weight loss and diabetes. I missed her point.

Later, she came over to where I was sitting and said, "I meant that you look happier than I have ever seen you before." Then I understood. People who love others want them to be happy. They are pleased to see it.

The second objective is to help church leaders particularly denominational officers both clergy and laity to think deeply, biblically, spiritually, and lovingly about what it means to restore any servant of God to health. For too long, Christians have assumed it is best to hide our problems. The last thing I needed was to be hidden. I needed help in learning to live again.

Living again is possible. Addiction is not the end of the world. As I like to say, the only true "rock bottom" in addiction is the bottom of the grave. Until then, recovery is possible with the proper medical, mental, and spiritual help.

Ask for it.

I Am a Wreck

"My name is Don, and I am a drunken pastor!"

"Did you say, 'drunken bastard?'" Everyone in the room laughed. I did, too.

The chaplain during Spiritual said, "That's what I thought he said, too." Everyone laughed again.

It was funny. But I was tired of it all. I was over the routine. I was disgusted with the program. I was a week short of leaving, and I could not wait to get out of there. My insurance had replied that my last week of the twenty-eight-day in patient stay would be covered. My counselor told me it was good news. I could imagine myself in a scenario where the same counselor would send me to the Billing department to talk about what would happen if my insurance would not pay.

I pictured some faceless billing director explaining that I would have to find some credit somewhere to get money to cover the final seven days. I would smile sheepishly, slowly shake my head with regret, and explain that there was nothing I could do. Then they would send me home. My wife or my dad would come to get me. I would sign some papers and be free of this six-week ordeal.

I was told the insurance agreed to pay. Despite my fantasy otherwise, I could have told them my insurance would pay. So, I had one more week, and nothing felt right about it. I wondered again, "How did I get into this mess?"

The answer to the question was simple. I was afraid I would die. I had been sick for several months. I was told after several tests that I had type 2 diabetes, a gallbladder "full of sludge," a non-obstructive stone in each kidney, and a fatty liver. These are all symptoms of alcoholism at a dangerous stage. No one said that though. I was lying about my drinking. I was lying to myself about my drinking. I hated my life. I wanted out. But I feared I was on my way out . . . permanently . . . if I didn't do something. One day during this struggle, the telephone rang.

It was my district superintendent, Jim. He needed to have a, as always overusing the word, conversation with me and another district superintendent. I knew what the conversation was about. I never could tell if Jim meant to be subtle and just could not pull it off. He mentioned my ministry, my family, and my life before hanging up. It was going to be an intervention.

Oh, what a horrible sounding word. Intervention is supposed to mean someone who cares about you is intervening in your life with other people who care about you. The objective of the action of intervening is a change, of course. I saw the sword of Damocles beginning to waver before it fell. What was I going to do?

I was going to tell the truth. That was all I could do. I was not the only one who asked that question either. Both my wife and my dad asked me. I gave them the same answer. One may well ask, how I could be clear-headed enough to make that decision? I do not know. I knew what I was going to do as soon as I poured myself another glass of brandy. I took a large gulp of the sweetly burning liquid as I nodded to myself knowing it was the way to go.

I was in a near-panic mode too. The panic was probably what made me take an easy out. I know that sounds strange. The easy way out of a situation avoids the consequences of the truth. I was avoiding the consequences of the lie. Oh, yes, I could lie about my drinking. I could do it and muster every bit of smug sincerity or faux outrage I would need depending on the situation at hand. But my alcohol-soaked brain could not settle on what I would say to answer the next question. Knowing that the first question was going to be some variation of, "are you drinking too much alcohol," was easy enough to figure out. But what would the next statement be? Would it be another opportunity to come clean or continue the lie? And then what would happen next? I could not predict the following steps well enough to know what I would do next. I could not strategize. The truth was the only option. And since it was the only option, and I needed help to cut down my drinking, it was the best option to get that help.

I woke up that morning with all the problems associated with heavy drinking the previous day. I experienced tremors and nausea. I drank some coffee with my regular half-and-half to have something on my stomach. I took my medicines, watched the news, and watched the clock until it was time to leave. But I left early thinking I needed extra time. I could not keep anything solid down. I could not tell if it was from withdrawal or nerves. I took two bottles of peach tea with me. I would drive with my left hand despite the tremor and drink the tea with my right hand which did not shake as badly. I dressed simply for the meeting, jeans, casual shoes, and a collared pullover. Since I was nauseous, I took another shirt in case I had to vomit.

I drank the first sixteen-ounce bottle of peach tea on that trip. I arrived early since I did not need to stop. I walked into the facility and was shown a room where I could wait. There were small bottles of water on the table. I wished to be somewhere else and for something stronger to drink. My stomach was hurting.

It was a room with overhead lighting that a friend of mine calls institutional. I do not like recessed ceiling lights with long fluorescent tubes. I hate opening those things. I hate even more replacing the tubes. Circular tables like the ones in the room are not pleasing, either. The chair, at least, was comfortable. The receptionist gave me directions to the restroom. I wondered if there would be any sympathy for me if I was found throwing up into the toilet. Sympathy, I was sure, was not on anyone's mind. My decision to tell the truth did not keep me from wanting to avoid the meeting where I had to tell it. After I returned to the room, the superintendents came in, and Jim closed the door.

Jim sat next to me as Lana sat across the table. We talked about a few matters including my family and my health. Jim led the conversation. I soon realized Lana's role was to be witness to an unrecorded interrogation. Knowing the roles people fill helps one strategize. It is how I kept juggling my life. I began to think I misunderstood the intention of the meeting when Jim came to it. "Don, given all of your stress and health problems, are you, in any way, self-medicating?" I kept my eyes on him throughout the question.

"Yes." I said almost immediately.

"How?" He asked.

"I've been drinking mostly hard liquor." I replied. I saw relief come over each of their faces. Jim pressed on.

"Are there any substances other than alcohol you are using?"

"No. Nothing illegal." I said and then hastily added, "And nothing I am prescribed right now is addictive, no opioids or other narcotics."

The conversation continued. Most of my fears of having to go on medical leave or being suspended from ministry dissipated. We agreed that I would call our conference counselor to get a recommendation for a drug and alcohol counselor near where I lived.

Before our prayer, Lana said something unexpected. "Thank you for being honest, Don."

I shook my head, "There is no point in lying."

"You wouldn't believe the number of people who have," she said.

The strategic alcoholic mind did not stop. "I thought about it. I decided this was the way to get help."

They asked if I was staying for lunch. I begged off saying I probably could not keep anything down. I took the bottle of water and drank it on the way home. I was under scrutiny now. Yet, I had my job, and I had a task to perform. I went home and poured myself some brandy.

That same day I made the call to the person temporarily serving in the role of conference counselor. She found a counselor for me in Jefferson City. I made the call and arranged an appointment. Then I called the district office to keep them informed. During this time, I continued drinking. The difficulty I had was that I thought I was tapering off.

Anyone who asked me was told, "I am drinking less." I told myself that and believed it. But I was not drinking less. Nor was I drinking more than I had been. I was drinking just as much. I may have been starting a little later. I thought so. But nothing changed. The real question is why did I not realize it?

When I could reflect on what was going on with me, I knew that my intervention meeting with Jim and Lana had been a meeting where I had experienced grace. I was given mercy for telling the truth. Yet I was only telling the truth that was easy for me to tell. I was lying to myself in other ways. The alcoholic paranoia was not abating either. I was easily upset by everything that seemed to go wrong. I was expecting another shoe to drop.

The counselor in Jefferson City informed me that my desire to learn how to drink responsibly was not going to happen. "Alcoholics do not get training in any way to curtail or lessen their consumption of booze," he said. There really is no cutting down. Alcoholics often assume they are merely heavy drinkers and believe they are mistakenly considered by other people to be alcoholics. As one church member said to me, "My definition of an alcoholic was someone who couldn't pay for his own drinks." In short, most people think the problem is a lack of discipline. Addiction goes so deep into the psyche that it alters the personality of the addict. This fact explains the "dry drunk" problem where one acts like a drunk in every way except for drinking and inebriation. Dry drunks make themselves and everyone else around them just as miserable as an actively drinking alcoholic.

A week later, Jim asked if he could come by on Saturday morning to discuss the situation with my wife and me. I told him what I thought would be a good time.

I was not looking forward to that meeting. So, I had a drink or two before he arrived. When he showed up, he sat on the sofa. My wife sat on the chair next to him. I sat across from her.

"I wonder how it has been going tapering off on your drinking?" He asked.

"I am doing alright," I said. "I am drinking three bottles of brandy a week."

"More like five," my wife said.

"Five?" I asked. "Really?"

She nodded, affirming it.

I puzzled over the number. I was sure it was only three.

Jim began again. "What I wanted to talk to you about is that Lilly had called me before we talked that time with Lana and said she had smelled alcohol on your breath." He paused allowing me to process that. "I propose we call her now and the four of us get into the place where we need to be."

Lilly was the Pastor-Parish Relations Committee (PPRC) Chair for both of my congregations. She is also a Nurse Practitioner. We agreed. He dialed the number and set his phone on the coffee table with the speaker on. She answered.

"Lilly? This is Jim Tallent. I am here with Don. He wants to tell you something important."

He nodded to me. I nodded back. I never liked talking to someone with the phone on speaker mode. Was I talking too loud or not loud enough? That day I did not want to be loud at all. I felt my privacy was being violated. I leaned forward in my chair.

"Can you hear me?" I asked.

"Yes," she said.

"Good," I began. "You know I have been having these health issues for a few months now. And I have been drinking hard liquor to help with the problems." There was some truth in that. "And I have been drinking way too much. I understand you have noticed that."

"Yes." She replied.

Jim jumped back into the conversation. "Don has begun seeing a counselor for his drinking and his doctor for the other issues. We just wanted to let you know so that all of us would be on the same page, so to speak."

She thanked him and then added. "I know that in my work that drinking only makes diabetes and gallbladder troubles worse. I would advise any patient I had to stop as soon as they could."

Jim closed the call saying, "I think we are all in a better place than we were when we started." He then left, offering a prayer for all of us.

I went upstairs to take a nap. After I woke up, I looked for something to watch on television and drank the rest of the day.

My son's girlfriend was going to visit during Holy Week. I wanted to stop drinking before then. If I could stop drinking altogether as the PPRC chair advised, then I would continue to see the counselor and work on staying sober. In other words, I decided I should stop drinking and stay stopped. I chose another Saturday, St. Patrick's Day, to stop.

It did not end well.

The night before St. Patrick's Day, I awoke to some serious gut pain. I drank what remained of the last bottle of brandy that night. When I awoke the next morning, I was not feeling well. There was no shaking and nausea though. I sat on the porch that morning and drank my coffee. Then I ate breakfast. After a while, the withdrawal symptoms began.

I started shaking. Now, I had planned for this possibility. I had thought buying some "non-alcoholic" beer would help. These drinks contain only the slightest amount of alcohol. I heard that alcoholics were told to avoid them because even a small amount can cause a relapse. My thinking went in the opposite direction. I was banking on the idea that the small amount could help my withdrawal symptoms. It did not work. I could not hold a glass or the bottle without spilling some, much less try to drink it.

I went upstairs to the bedroom. My wife followed me. I felt cold. My whole body was shaking by this time as though I was freezing to death. I wrapped myself in a blanket. I was shaking so hard I could barely talk. My wife lay against me outside the blanket. She said I felt hot, like I had a bad fever.

I went back downstairs and tried drinking water because I was experiencing reflux and the cough that comes with it. My wife started to go take a shower in the downstairs bathroom. I ran past her to vomit. The regurgitation helped lessen the shaking. I drank some water and then the non-alcoholic beer. It was room temperature by that time. I went back upstairs and laid down again.

The withdrawal worsened. I was on my way to being sick to my stomach again. When my wife came in to check on me, she checked me for a fever. I had a small gain in temperature. The shaking was violent now.

"Do you want me to get you something?" She asked. Her voice sounded very deliberate, even, and very annoyed.

"You mean from the liquor store?" I asked, still shaking.

"Yes." Her tone was the same as when one asked her about a topic that she thought she had already explained.

"No." I replied defensively. "I just have to get through this."

She got up and went downstairs.

This attempt is called "white knuckling" by recovering addicts. The image is that of a person hanging from a cliff with only a precarious grip on a protruding rock keeping him from falling. Picture the strain in the muscles of the hand leaving the skin stretched over the knuckles as the hand slips from the rock.

A few minutes later my alcoholic mind decided to find its salvation. I had a mild stroke ten years before and a hospital stay because of it. I did not want another one. Managing to roll to a sitting position, I took a few deep breaths and stood. I went back downstairs and asked her to get me a small bottle of brandy. She left immediately.

I waited until she got back and drank two glasses of it to make the withdrawals stop. I swore I would never try that again. The problem remained. If I cannot stop, how can I taper down? The good news was that I had an appointment with my counselor in just a few days.

I went to that small office again and talked to my counselor. He suggested sports drinks for replacing the fluids from my almost daily vomiting spells. "When I was in the rehab unit at the hospital, we went through a cabinet full of Gatorade in two days," he said.

"We need to bring in your medical doctor now," he said. "It is not recommended that you try going cold turkey again. You could cause a seizure or worse." I mentioned the stroke I had years before. He nodded and said, "You can withdraw from heroin and feel like you are going to die but won't. Withdrawing from alcohol can kill you."

It was the first time I heard that. I knew people, even family members, who had stopped drinking. I never knew about any symptoms either. The idea that a person could die from drinking too much—alcohol poisoning—that I knew about. Dying by quitting? I let that thought simmer for a while. Later, I told my wife that must be the meaning of the phrase "dying for a drink." I had an appointment with my doctor during Holy Week. I decided I would tell him. My son's girlfriend was about to arrive. I wanted to keep from acting like a complete jerk to her like I had done before and had since apologized. I kept my distance from her.

It almost worked, too.

Unfortunately, a day came when I had to bail out of teaching a class because I became sick to my stomach. Vomiting during class was not an option. Yet I began vomiting a few hours before the class began. My son's girlfriend asked something I considered none of her business. "How much have you had?"

"I want to tell you," I began saying to her, "Before you got here, I tried to stop. I got so sick we worried about it. I am seeing my doctor tomorrow. That is what the counselor advised. Don't start criticizing!"

She apologized and backed off. What I said was true. Unfortunately, the way I expressed the truth was loud and threatening.

The next morning, I went to see the doctor. I had not seen him in some time. I was able to be reinstated as a patient. I took that as a good sign. I went to the office building. It was familiar. The outside of the building had not changed much. Inside it was a different experience.

I remembered a pharmacy where now a lab is housed. It was on the right-hand side as I entered. I remembered the staircase I saw to my left. The long front desk for the receptionists had only changed slightly. Only one receptionist looked familiar. As a United Methodist minister living the every-three-year reassignments, I was used to learning new names in a short time. The waiting area had changed considerably. I could no longer see the nurse as she walked out into the doorway leading to the examination rooms. The waiting area was noisy. I listened intently for my name to be called. I did not have to wait long.

"Don Jones," a nurse called out to the room. She correctly assumed I went by my middle name. Points for her, I thought. She led me through the door. When she weighed me and measured my height, I was the heaviest I had ever been in my life. Then I followed her to the exam room for a blood pressure check. I was surprised to learn my pressure was a little lower than normal. But I was beginning withdrawal again. Despite my shaking, it was easy for the nurse to take my blood pressure. The oxy-pulse monitor recorded my resting heart rate was 102 beats per minute.

The doctor came in and greeted me like an old friend. We shook hands. He asked about my family. I have always liked him. He is a good man, and he is also very discreet. He was once a Navy doctor. I wondered how he would react to my problem. I assumed with his service he had to have seen it before. I was right.

He examined me and asked a few health questions. It was soon over. He sat down and asked, "Is there anything else?" I assumed that he wanted to hear me say it.

"I am a wreck," I began. "I drink most of the day every day." Then I told him about trying to quit and the problem with withdrawal. I also told him about what the counselor had said.

He replied, "This disease can happen to anyone. It does not matter your social status or your job or background or any of those things people often judge to be the problem."

I nodded, indicating I was listening.

He went on, "So, you're sitting here shaking and sweating with a definitely high heart rate," he checked his tablet to see the number again. "So, we have a couple of options. We can send the medicine home with you." I liked the sound of that. "But you have to keep up with the stepping-down process. And, of course, you can't drink while on this medicine. You must be monitored." He paused and then said, "I prefer to put you in the hospital for a few days. We can do that today if you want, or we can wait until next week."

I quickly made a bad decision for good reasons. Easter Sunday was coming in four days. There were a lot of activities in which I was expected to take part. Plus, my son's girlfriend was still with us.

"Would it be all right to wait until Monday after Easter?" I asked.

He agreed and said he would begin the paperwork. I went home and explained the plan to everyone. Saturday came with my son and his girlfriend going to the airport. Before they left, she hugged me and said, "Do your best." I made it to all the Saturday activities and the Sunrise service Sunday morning. But withdrawal was so bad, I started drinking after the Sunrise service. I got sick over breakfast and did not make it to the other worship times. I alternated between sleeping and drinking the rest of the day. That night I wrote in a notebook pouring out all my anger at God and the church for how awful my life had been. I was not happy with anything in my life.

The next morning my wife drove me to the doctor's office. I expected to be immediately sent to the hospital from there. Of course, it did not work out that way. The nurse said no beds were available. She explained we would be called by the hospital when a room was open. We decided to go to lunch and wait. Then my withdrawal symptoms began and rapidly got worse. After lunch, I began gagging and coughing, signaling I was about to be violently ill. We decided to go to my father's house.

Dad was not home, but I had a key. We went inside where I found a bottle of brandy and poured myself a glass. I got the first drink down. It helped the nausea. Dad came home and found us there. I told him what was going on. We talked while I drank a second glass and began a third. The hospital called during my third drink and told me what time to check in. I finished my drink. My tremors and other symptoms of withdrawal were satisfied. I finished the rest of the bottle before it was time to go. My wife drove me to the hospital.

I walked in and signed the necessary forms. I was drunk. But I was steady. I could have walked to the elevator and gone to my room. Hospital policy, since I was being admitted, required that I travel by wheelchair. Once in the room, I changed into my pajama pants and put on the hospital gown. The nurses and technicians came in to hook me up to a heart monitor, take blood, and put an IV in my arm for saline solution to keep me from becoming more dehydrated. I could rest for a while. Later, a nurse came in to tell me more about what they intended to do. They were not starting the withdrawal meds yet, because I came in drinking.

I started to say if the hospital had done everything properly, I would not have needed to drink. I did not say it though. A few more hours had to go by before they would give me the appropriate drug. I watched TV and talked to my wife until she left. It was her spring break week. She had made plans to go hiking with another teacher. She had class work to finish. And she was working toward her master's degree. She left me with a few snacks and Gatorade. I had brought a copy of the Bible and *Alcoholics Anonymous*—what AA members call "the Big Book." I read some until an idea struck me.

I knew another United Methodist pastor who lived nearby. I heard some of his stories about recovering from alcoholism. I texted him and asked if he would come visit me. He replied that he could the next morning. I slept off and on through the first night.

Jeff arrived while I was reading my morning meditations. He sat down and asked, "What's going on?"

"Well," I began, "I am an alcoholic."

"Welcome to the club," he said.

He spent some time there with me as we talked about everything that had been going on with me. Jeff told me his story, and then he asked something I sort of expected.

"Don, I want to ask you something. Did you make a drunk post about the bishop?"

I was embarrassed. It was a shameful social media post. I did not realize it until the morning after I posted it. "Yes," I said.

"I thought so," he began. "What really surprised me was the number of people who agreed with what you said." He then laughed.

I laughed about it too. It was a form of gallows humor. In my case, I was laughing at my own misery and barely acknowledged it.

A caseworker came into my room later that day to ask me what my plans were after the hospital stay. I replied, "I am planning to go back to work and then start meetings." She asked if I had considered an inpatient facility or an intensive outpatient program (IOP). The fact was that neither option had crossed my mind. My education and training on the subject were minimal. "I started reading the Big Book," I explained.

She looked skeptical about my plan. She could not make me do anything, she said. Yet, she made it clear I was going to fail.

The rest of the day was uneventful. My father came by bringing some Gatorade and the newspaper. I watched television and took my meds. I was able to get around some. I walked around my room to the lavatory. I read. I talked on the phone. I did some social media stuff. My wife came by. I did not know that I was really getting weaker rather than stronger.

That night I woke up ill and began vomiting. I drank soda to settle my stomach the next morning. I was still vomiting and could not eat very much. I tried asking my wife to bring my laptop. I was unable to get her to understand what papers I needed in addition to the computer. I started vomiting during the call. "Just forget it and come on," I said gulping air to keep from vomiting.

The nurse came in to check my vitals. She remarked my temperature was up. She checked the IV needle. A knot was forming in that spot. Blood tests were ordered. Later, the nurse returned.

"Your sugar is too high. I have insulin for you. Do you normally take it?"

"No," I said. I was shaking. I was surprised to hear my sugar was high.

She brought in the CNA to help me stand while she gave me the injection. Then they helped me to the lavatory. I got back into bed with their help. After a while, a doctor came into my room. "It looks like we decreased the dosage of your withdrawal medicine too early. We think you have developed a blood clot because of the IV. And you have a staph infection. We are going to move you to CCU and bring Dr. Tan onto your case." He left.

I called my wife to tell her I was being moved. I let my friends on Facebook know. The IV needle was moved to my other arm.

I do not recall having any trouble sleeping. The unit nurse woke me and put me on oxygen. "You're having some apnea," she said. I slept the rest of the night.

I was taken that next day—Thursday—to the imaging department to check on the blood clot. I was moved back to a regular room, then Jim came to visit me. Time became more confusing then. I was confused enough already. I was supposed to be getting medical help to break the alcohol habit. Now I was in a potentially life-threatening situation. I had known a few people who had died with staph infections. Thankfully, I did not need more insulin. The doctor put me on a powerful antibiotic. There was a second IV bag for it. I would not be able to be back in the pulpit the following Sunday.

I told Jim when he sat in the chair next to my bed that we needed someone to fill in on Sunday. He had already thought of that and had more thoughts to share.

"I have already provided to have someone fill in for you the next six weeks," he said. He then paused for a moment. Seeing I did not answer, he continued, "Every medical person and recovery expert I have talked to says that the best way for anyone to recover from alcohol or drug addiction is a twenty-eight-day residential treatment. So, I have talked to Ken, the conference insurance director, and a member of the Fountain City church named Beth who said they can get you into Cornerstone for the twenty-eight-day program when you leave the hospital."

I did not like that idea at all. It sounded like being locked up in jail or a mental health facility of some kind. I knew about such places. Well, I knew some about them. My counselor instructed me to see the film *28 Days* starring Sandra Bullock. I ordered a DVD copy. But it had not arrived by the time I went to the hospital.

Jim was telling me that my earlier plan was being dismissed outright. It was evident in his mind the best chance meant the only way to recover.

He provided me with some phone numbers to call. I was also concerned about something else.

I was still working on my doctoral degree and in the middle of a New Testament course at the time. I had already received permission to miss a couple of classes. I did not want to quit that program to chase recovery which was what I thought I was in the hospital for to begin with. At the very least, I wanted to finish the semester.

I was brooding over this when another problem came up. Dr. Tan arrived after Tom left. She told me the situation. All I remember of it was her telling me, "Good luck," and then, seeing my copy of *Alcoholics Anonymous*, she gave a nod of her head toward it and said, "Good luck with that, too."

Any patient can tell you that the nurse is tasked with explaining what the next steps are. The doctor gives information. The nurse gives instructions. I could go home Friday . . . maybe. When I went home, I would be required to carry an IV bag and pump that would need changing every third day. I would be wearing that device for about fourteen days as it pumped the antibiotic into me. I had several concerns about this. None of them were rational.

I called Dave at Cornerstone about admission. I told him my two-week problem. It was indeed a problem.

"The medical staff won't allow you to be checked in with an IV bag and pump," he said. "What about intensive outpatient? Maybe I can do that instead?"

"No. You are not going to be checked in at all. I know you are in the hospital for detox now. But you will be required to spend some time in our detox facility to make sure you are not drinking."

That made no sense to me. I called Jim to tell him. He disliked a well-prepared plan being disrupted. "What if" became the words I hated most to hear. In our back-and-forth discussions Jim proposed a lot of scenarios by which I could possibly get into the inpatient treatment program right away. When I broached these with Dave, he shut every one of them down. Jim seemed to think I was just being difficult. Maybe even trying to get out of it all together. Unfortunately for me, Jim's anxieties were only going to get worse.

I went home the following day—Friday—with the bag and pump. Sunday, I drove back to the hospital to get the bag changed. Jim called every day. The recurring question was why was I not in Cornerstone? The answer was always the same. "I can't be admitted yet." I was not sure I would be admitted after I was done with the antibiotics. I shared this concern with Lilly at my church. "Don't worry," she said, "I keep a list of every place from here to Johnson City for my patients."

Spring break was over. I was alone much of the day at home. I had little to do. I answered Jim's calls. I fought the urge to drink. My anxieties grew. The urge to drink got worse. The tactical thinking began to get worse. Since I would have to spend time in detox when I went to treatment, why should I not get a bottle of brandy and start over? My more rational mind said, because it will hinder the antibiotic.

A few times I made extra trips to the hospital because the tube would break or detach from the IV bag. I learned how to best clip the tube to keep from having the medicine all over me and my clothes. It was after one of those I decided to meet Ken, the Conference insurance coordinator, in person, before I returned home. I was glad to catch him in his office.

I saw the elderly man who had spoken very gently to me on the phone. He was aware of my situation. He had told me over the phone that once I get out of treatment, I would need to get to work on myself. I would not be truly sober until I did that. I did not understand what he was talking about at the time.

I asked, "Does our conference policy cover a full month of inpatient treatment?"

"Yes," he replied.

"I had a conversation with someone who said they may only pay part of the cost. "How come our insurance pays full coverage?"

"Because we are self-funded like the railroad insurance," he began. "If Blue Cross rejects your claim for any reason, just call me and I'll tell them to cover it." Then he added. "They handle the paperwork, but we pay the bill." In my then seventeen years of ministry with the Holston Annual Conference of The United Methodist Church, I never learned what it meant to have self-funded insurance until then. I was not going to face a major medical bill by going into inpatient treatment. I could not afford it, but the Conference could. It was the first time I felt good about the whole issue.

"When will you be going to Cornerstone?" Jim asked.

Whatever the number of days it had been was the number of times I had answered this one question. "I have this pump for fourteen days. They will decide then if they are going to take it off me."

"Can you then go in that day?" he asked.

"The fourteenth day is a Saturday." I replied. "I do not know if they would make me wait until the following Monday to check-in. But I am sure they take people on Saturdays." Then he said the most annoying statement ever. "Well, I am just concerned that the people in the church are seeing you out in the yard or driving around town and wondering why you aren't working." It was nothing less than harassment. No one from the churches had broached that subject with me. And if they had with him, it was really none of their business. I had not asked to be out of the pulpit those weeks. Jim had decided that. He was having anxieties about a problem that was his own making, and he worried about how he might have to answer inquiring people who called him.

I could not help feeling angry because I was the one who was sick. I had an infection. I had the cravings to drink. I was trying to do my best. And I did not need the pressure from someone about whom a counselor has since said, "was more concerned about the church institution than you."

The next time I heard from him, he threatened me. I would either be in Cornerstone soon or be put on involuntary medical leave. I exploded.

I did not blow up on him. It was late in the evening. I was returning home from the hospital. I called my wife and told her to call him and explain that I was not taking any more calls from him. It was harassment. I am doing the best I can. He needs to stop. The reason I gave her to do it was that I would most certainly be out of a job when I was done saying exactly what was on my mind.

'Okay," she said. And she did it.

When I made it home, she told me what Jim had said. "I am sorry. I have never dealt with something like this before." Well, neither had I, and that fact was not being considered.

I was calm when I got home. "Perhaps, he should talk to someone who has," was all I said about it remembering Lana's statement about the number of people who had lied to them. Someone in authority should have known what to do.

The best part of being locked up, I thought then, would be that I would not have to deal with him for the next month. I planned that Saturday, with all arrangements being made, that if they took the pump off, I would check in right after to Cornerstone. And that is what I did.

Chapter 2

Bottled History

It is an obvious question to ask, "How does a pastor become an alcoholic?"
The question is more perplexing when long-term treatment for alcoholism
is said to involve "spiritual principles." If a pastor is not living according to
spiritual principles, then who is? The answer to that question is . . . lots of
people, including pastors.

I grew up in a fundamentalist church where a person is "one-drink
drunk." If a person takes a drink of alcohol, that person is now drunk. Yes, it
violates common sense. The argument is that the first drink begins the process of fogging the sensibilities of the person who drinks, I was told. A true
Christian should always be in possession of his or her faculties. Obviously,
this idea did not apply to people who were receiving a general anesthetic or
a narcotic for harsh pain. These activities were medical necessities. We even
saw movies where cowboys were given whiskey before one of the other
guys removed bullets from them. The problem involved someone drinking
socially or at home in secret. Plainly stated, someone who used alcohol
was violating the requirements of Holy Scripture. There were two problems
with this assertion.

The first problem is that all examples we were given from the Bible
involved being intoxicated. There were no demonstrated violations of divine law where a person had a glass of wine (or two) with dinner. It should
surprise no one that this focus on intoxication was the actual root of the
"one-drink drunk" rule. If the Bible only condemns "drunkenness," then
one gets "drunk" on the first drink. This is an example of reading what one

wants to see in the text. The technical term is *eisegesis*. It is the opposite of *exegesis,* which is about reading a text to draw out information. To read into the text a meaning that is not within the text itself is a violation of fundamentalist faith. And yet fundamentalism has a long history in such interpretation.

The second problem is it calls into question the nature of God. Alcohol is a natural substance. The process of fermentation happens without any human interference. Humans can either arrest that process or make it more efficient. But that does not take away from the fact that alcohol is literally part of the created order. The first chapter of Genesis ends with God declaring all the creation "very good." God cannot have created anything evil in and of itself. It is a divine impossibility. If alcohol is evil in itself, then the scripture would claim that God, who is goodness itself, is the author of evil.

The ancient heresy we call Gnosticism held that all things of the Spirit were holy whereas all things of the created order were unclean and thereby created by a lesser being than the God revealed by Jesus. Human beings were spirits trapped in unclean bodies. Gnostics then differed on what that belief meant for Christian conduct.

A Christian then may use alcohol but may not abuse it. The use of alcohol is regulated in scripture. It is not forbidden except for those under certain vows. People with special vows could decide not to use some "creature" of the created order. Yet it could not be forbidden for everyone. The use of all sources of life are regulated in the Bible. This is the very reason fundamentalists often declare the Bible as the guide for faith and practice. The Bible can still be misinterpreted by fundamentalists (and often is). And so, a strange metamorphosis takes place from the Bible being the rule to the interpretation of certain fundamentalist teachers being the rule.

Another issue occurring in fundamentalist culture is the need to ignore the rules. Essentially, fundamentalism and conservative evangelicalism are antinomian. I understand the confusion a person may experience here. Living according to the rules and teachings is important. However, there are more important aspects to peoples' lives than living according to those rules. The Southern Baptist Convention ruled that women are meant to be home makers and mothers, according to God's plan, and should not work outside the home. Most Southern Baptist families agreed that this was the teaching of the Bible. But they did not alter their lifestyles to accommodate the teaching. Why? Because it was *impractical.* The household budgets of these families could not function without having two incomes. Life may have been survivable if the husbands and fathers of these families had incomes that equaled the amount being brought in by a two-income family. The Southern Baptist Convention did not take this issue into account.

Passively ignoring the rules laid down by the fundamentalist culture becomes a primary feature of that culture. The reasons given for ignoring the rules often are about practicality. The other reasons usually involve mental gymnastics that show why the standard interpretations do not apply in the situations involved. Fundamentalist Christians are often violent to each other, despise their neighbors, partake of alcohol and illegal drugs, indulge in pornography, lie, cheat, and steal. And they condemn all these sins. The veneer of righteousness is maintained by making certain declarations from the pulpits and church classrooms that there is mercy, forgiveness, and charity for those people who commit all sins. But there must be one or two sins that are wholly and completely unforgivable. Their primary function is to set a boundary. They mark who is in the culture and who is outside it.

When a person is a participant or an advocate for any of the unforgivable sins, then they are assigned the place of outsider. All the sins that fundamentalists condemn, participate in, and forgive themselves for can be condemned in the outsider. As one church member told me after the 2016 Presidential election, "No Christian can support abortion." Another way to phrase it is, no person can be a Christian unless they are in the fundamentalist camp.

Charlatans learn this rule very quickly. They then find their way into the good graces of the most sincere fundamentalist believers. Such situations are appalling to any thinking person fundamentalist or not. People in such sick situations become antibodies touched by the infection.

My ministry was within this context. Every church I served fit the profile of the fundamentalist culture I have described. Every congregation perpetuated it and suffered from it. None of them ever got over it. They are all dying from it, and there is nothing to be done about it. The tragedy is that those church officials in every denomination who recognize the problem will not publicly name it and condemn it.

The United Methodist Church uses what is called "the appointment system" for placing pastors in churches. Congregations do not choose their clergy leaders. Many congregations resent that fact. Those congregations do not face the problem of having no clergy person when needed that their neighbor churches using "the call system" have. Each system has its problems and benefits. Clergy in the appointment system find that they are not endlessly sending out sermon recordings and resumes. They usually leave one place with another church waiting to receive them. Often these clergy members do not have a choice in placement or compensation package. Mismatches happen even when a congregation's needs are evaluated with the skills of the available clergy.

I often felt there was a note in the bishop's office that said "congregation fixer" beside my name. Once I left seminary, it appeared to me that every congregation or multi-congregation charge had some problem in administration and/or leadership. I began thinking my job on any pastoral moved was to repair a situation I did not cause. Once during an introductory meeting with the PPRC a lady spoke up, "Did the superintendent tell you that you are coming to a congregation that has had problems?" I replied, "It won't be the first time." When I related this story at the church, I was preparing to leave the PPRC chair said, "Did they have any idea of what you walked into here?"

Congregations usually blame their problems on the previous pastors. Sometimes they are correct. I harbor no illusions that I have not been blamed for problems. In fact, I am sure I caused some. The leadership in my Annual Conference knew congregations blamed their pastors. It did not matter. If the congregation's apportionment payments were restored with attendance and budget increased, a ministry was considered successful. I moved every three or four years on average, and it was often the same story. Some superintendents tell me they asked for me specifically because of the needs and prejudices of the congregation. It was flattering. But my salary was cut three times on such moves. My children did not get the best public schools. My wife could not hold a teaching job. We struggled as a family. And I started drinking because of the psychological pain involved.

There was also physical pain involved. I suffered a light stroke in 2008. I was forty-two years old. After that, my arthritis pain began and gradually got worse. Old people used to refer to alcohol as "rheumatism medicine." Booze eases the pain. It does not cure arthritis. Ultimately, alcohol worsens the inflammation. I could manage what I was doing. I did not find my work very challenging. The job, however, was another issue entirely.

The fundamentalist culture has devastated congregations. During the early 1990s religious statisticians reported that the growing congregations identified as "evangelical." Large warehouse-style churches that did not identify with any denomination with simple messages and music presentations that resembled secular concerts appeared to be the churches of the future. These congregations often billed themselves as "different" than the churches that were the backbone of the fundamentalist culture. This marketing was often a bait-and-switch exercise that brought people that were somewhat disaffected by traditional churches. Over time it became apparent that the so-called "contemporary" churches were not growing. They were experiencing a phenomenon best described as "swelling." People flocked to either a favored performance by the musicians or a particularly charismatic pastor. If there was a change of one or the other, the participants went to another church of the same stripe looking for a similar experience. One person told of a family that had settled in four different churches in as many years. The contemporary churches tended to cater to the tastes of baby boomers. Despite attempts to form church small groups there was little success in personal growth, accountability, or other intangibles. One church statistician stated, at one of our gatherings, the famed Willow Creek Church had a back door where former members looking for spiritual growth and disciplined life found their way to Roman Catholicism, Eastern Orthodoxy, or the Episcopal Church.

Denominational leaders who supped at the table of the contemporary church model never got past the idea even when the evidence showed that its time was over. The churches that got branded as traditional, which made up the fundamentalist culture, did not like the contemporary style of music (what's wrong with the old favorites?). By and large, they had no intention of going that route. The churches resisted, and the culture remained. These congregations began to see themselves as outsiders.

Larger congregations with more money found ways to accommodate everyone. They developed two distinct services. One worship time was dedicated to the traditional model. Another time (and often space) was set aside for the contemporary model. This arrangement remains in many churches but there is one drawback. Contemporary worship is more expensive to put on than the traditional one. It demands a larger share of the congregational budget. But the contemporary service does not pay for itself. The people who attend the traditional service primarily pay for both services even though the contemporary service has higher attendance.

I once served a church where the members sought to become contemporary with a new building and grand plans. It was assumed that new people from nearby subdivisions would attend and bring the money to pay for it. However, a check of the patterns of giving to the congregation showed that most of the people who came from the subdivisions either gave noth-ing or substantially less than the "old timers." There was no way to increase the budget to do what people said they wanted. No matter how much "real talk" was offered, no one listened. Now the building stands empty with the words "for sale" on the marquee.

The small, rural, traditional churches long for things to be the way they once were. They want the well-attended events they once had (Vaca-tion Bible Schools, revival meetings, and full buildings on Sundays) as well as the people who have walked away. These desires are impossible to fulfill. One colleague said to me that he managed to bring in new members and some of the ones who had previously left. The newcomers usually stayed and became involved while the others left again after a while. He asked if it was a waste of time. Fundamentalist culture makes it "a waste of time" by granting such persons the assurance that they are insiders who will always have a place. No one will condemn "those who are ours." The problem is impossible to overcome even when hard evidence is given to the lay officers of the congregation. The attitude of "we know what we think, and you won't change our minds" flourishes in most congregations. Many pastors yearn for the opportunity to start their own churches. Such churches would be free from the established patterns of authority and processes of governance that tend to stymie the plans of the pastors. Sometimes such start-ups work with a heavy investment of money and time. Often, they do not. The pastors usually lack the ability to build and sustain the new congregations. Such skills are difficult to train in a person. But there is one other problem I have experienced other than the established patterns and processes I have just described. The larger portion of the members of congregations refuse to be taught.

Sitting in an annual meeting of the PPRC of the church whose building went up for sale, I was astounded by the statement, "You preach like you are trying to teach us something." I really should not have been surprised. I spoke about this problem with the conference counselor who said, "They just want you to confirm their prejudices." Teaching is not valued in most congregations. A friend remarked to me, "Only fundamentalists want Bible study." Another more conservative colleague complained that it was easier to get people to attend a church–sponsored trip to the baseball park than it is to get them to Bible study. These are both common complaints from pastors.

I want to know what is true and to teach it. I am not impressed by showmanship, emotional manipulation, or other gimmicks used by those who appear to be successful for a time. I cannot claim that Jesus spoke to me. Being Protestant, the Blessed Virgin, ignores me. God never spoke to me. The Holy Spirit never laid anything "on my heart" even when I thought it happened. I heard other preachers talk about such things. They were not always televangelists nor did they all have large congregations or mega-churches. I did not immediately doubt their experiences unless the spiritual experience described was contrary to the teachings of the scriptures. I often envied those people who claimed spiritual experience. I wanted to have these experiences. I thirsted for them. I made mental efforts to recall my dreams to see if any of them could be visions. Sometimes I fancied they were indeed more than simply my subconscious at work. It was to no avail. God has never spoken to me. A New Age practitioner told me I was "blocked." A Pentecostal friend told me I needed "deliverance." I must say if God cannot get through my mental blocks or is somehow less powerful than a demon possessing my soul, then God is not worthy of worship.

I was at a standstill. The psychological pain was immense. I invested heavily in an education to allow me to do a job that was impossible to do in my setting. I resented the job. I resented everything about my life. Worst of all, I was not allowed to leave it behind. The mental barriers were in place. I could blame lots of people. I blamed my family most of all. My then wife worried about the family's security. I worried about my own. The unimaginable irony was that my continued and increased abuse of alcohol jeopardized that desired security more.

What would I have done otherwise? I do not know. Drinking was one task to which I would devote myself. I wondered about writing full time. Such a career did not bring health insurance, a dwelling, or a position in the larger community. I would still have the problems. The biggest problem would continue to be with me no matter what I did.

The first step is, "We admitted we were powerless over alcohol–that our lives had become unmanageable." I have a hard time admitting I am powerless over anything. My family and community told me I could do practically anything I wanted to do. Who else could have gone to seminary full-time, managed three churches on a circuit, and taken care of a family with small children? Who else could lead the rebuilding of a church that only had seven people in attendance on my first Sunday, and work full time on night shift at a factory job? If I could do all that, I could control my intake of alcohol.

My biggest excuse for drinking more and more was that I could not manage myself in the situations I describe earlier in this chapter. I was born too late and had missed the "great years" of church work. My ambitions were still there, bordering on bravado. I was trying to find an escape. I tried something else to get out of my boredom with my work and feelings of loneliness even with my family around me. I decided to study for a Doctorate.

Study was one aspect of my life and career I was good at doing. I am blessed with a good memory. I like learning ideas and concepts. I enjoy understanding how a scholar's argument or theory works. I love books even though I am not fond of academic writing. I recall struggling, as a young student. with mathematics for years, until one day, while trudging through a high school course, the symbols of equations began to stand for words. I was given the key to the door. I enjoyed trigonometry and calculus more than first year algebra for that reason alone. In other words, I am usually confident that, if I work at it, I will figure out the problem and the solution to it. This attitude did not mean I always got the correct answer. I could be wildly wrong on occasion. I would know how the method worked, though, I could be corrected.

I got my Master of Divinity degree on someone else's dime. Emory University is a great place for scholarships. The Candler School of Theology is good for training students for to be Christian clergy. The scholarships I received as a student there paid for all tuition, fees, and books. I felt an obligation, too, when going to classes because I was taking so many people with me. They were my family and friends who were supportive, my congregations who put up with me being gone for most of the time, the Holston Conference leadership who were investing in me, and the people who provided the money for me to attend. I thought of all of them walking into classes with me. My theology did not allow me to think I was "bringing God" with me. I saw myself as continually attempting to get to the divine person. I graduated in 2002. Then fourteen years later, I returned.

I was surprised how lazy and complacent I had become. I did not find pastoral ministry intellectually challenging. It was emotionally challenging to be sure. My physical health was suffering. Booze was making all of it worse. My intellectual pursuits had been put aside for a very long time. I was resentful about it. A friend says I was wasted by not having the proper stimulation for my mind. My research, reading, listening, and writing skills for academic work had become corroded. The first course in my doctoral work, which was an introduction for all students, was designed for someone like me who needed to grease the gears. I needed to do that work and be held accountable for doing it.

I felt like an old slacker when I introduced myself to my fellow students. Many of these people were much younger. The few who were close to my age were second-career clergy people. And there was one student in our group who I considered an overachiever. After she described the many ministerial and educational tasks of her life, I felt like I needed a nap. One younger member of the class who had been raised on *Harry Potter* jokingly asked the overachiever if she possessed a "time-turner" that allowed her to squeeze out more time to do all the jobs at which she had been successful. And this student was only one example of those who were in my academic cohort. All the other students were capable of doing the work of ministry and the work of practical theological reflection that would be involved. The next three years were going to be very different from the ones when I got my Master's degree.

The course work, after the rocky start, fit in well with the lifestyle I was living. I could read, write, compare, and do my job for the most part with a tumbler in my right or left hand. I got very used to the idea of being on the computer with a glass of brandy next to me. I had thought brandy was a better choice than whiskey. It was thicker and easier to stomach. And by drinking it, I would not get as drunk. I must have gotten that false idea from somewhere in fiction. The whiskey I occasionally bought and the brandy I always bought were both forty proof.

Reading my assignments and working for class did two important things for me. The first was that I found again the desire to put more work in my sermons for church. I was being given new resources and new insights into my regular studies that helped me produce my sermons and the twice a year scripture study programs I used in the church setting. It was a small group that attended the studies. The feedback I got from the classes I taught indicated that they were appreciated and useful. I had already instituted an Evening Prayer service the nights of the studies. These classes became more in depth and usable to the church people who attended the class.

The second thing that my studies helped me with was giving me more opportunities to drink. I could drink more and earlier on the days I "just had to do my homework." It was a wonderfully deceptive excuse. It only worked on the one person I needed it to work on. And that person was me. I was my best audience. When the words on the page became too blurry, I took a nap to help some of the inebriation pass. I would wake up an hour and a half to two hours later, pour another drink, and get back to "work." I am certain the time to finish these tasks was being dragged out this way. It did not matter. I had taken on the doctoral program in consultation with the PPRC and my district superintendent. If I did not make it to the hospital often enough or some other pastoral visit, it would have to be all right. I was doing most of my other jobs.

I justified myself with certain thoughts. I led two worship services every Sunday, preaching at both. I showed up most Saturday mornings to the Clothes Closet even though I was not expected to stay the whole time. I taught my class. I served on the Board of Directors for the Cocke County Food Bank. I was active in the community and attended community events. I organized community worship times. I kept up with the church officers and the tedious paperwork involved. I read the financial reports and attended church council meetings for both congregations. I supported special events put on by the church. I offered ideas and plans. I made reports on my activities to the quarterly PPRC. I attended district clergy meetings. The Doctor of Ministry program allowed me to be exempted from all but the required Conference education events. And, in what became the most important part in the life of the churches to me, I attended and participated in Wonderful Wednesday.

Wonderful Wednesday was an after-school program that brought local children from the nearby elementary school to our church annex for about two hours once a week. These students were from kindergarten through the fifth grade. Working with those children was fun, heartbreaking, rewarding, and frustrating at the same time. I made sure, if there was any way possible, to be in attendance. When the program grew from nine children each week to more than thirty, my district superintendent joked that it was the "third church" on my circuit.

The after-school program became the focus of my doctoral project. I had not planned for it to happen. I first considered another program I was involved with to be the focus of my project. Then something happened making the chemicals in my brain converge on an idea.

One young girl came late to Wonderful Wednesday. I said, "I was beginning to think you weren't coming." Her response was, "I am not going to miss Sunday School."

Sunday school.

On Wednesday.

At that moment I realized that none of the adults involved in the after-school program had discussed and likely never considered how the children viewed the program. We had a vague notion about reaching out to school-aged children. We offered a snack meal to them when they arrived, homework help, a time for stories and lessons taken from the Bible, a time to pray, and a time to play. We hoped we would help them in these areas of their life and their personal growth. That one student's statement prompted me to ask, "What did the children understand about what was taking place?"

The girl had said, "Sunday school." What was that anyway? If a church provides Sunday school to children, what is going on then?

The church where I grew up had a large education program for children and youth. We had been divided up by our public-school grades into classes each Sunday. Many Sunday school teachers had to be persuaded or cajoled into serving. Other teachers served because they always had. For instance, one married couple always taught the class for four-year-old children. I believe they even considered it their mission in life. However all the teachers were brought to serving, it was much more fun for us than going upstairs to the worship service. I am thankful to them for the time they donated to us.

While I was in ministry, many of the congregations I served had few to no children for Sunday school even if the children came to worship services. Why? There are answers unique to situations and families, but it all came to the same thing. Parents and grandparents just did not believe it was worth the effort to have their children in Sunday school. The after-school program differed in one major aspect. It was a convenience to the families who often needed someone to watch their children until they got home from work.

The lay leader of the congregation approached me one Sunday morning and exclaimed, "Twenty in Wonderful Wednesday last week, twenty-five this week. Don't tell us we don't have a children's program." Another church member, I was told, regarded it as "glorified baby-sitting." He was corrected by someone who had seen what we did with the students each week.

Even though I was not sure about whether that girl attended Sunday school regularly, she knew what it was. It was about church. It had something to do with the church. The church had something to do with God. My district superintendent was correct. Wonderful Wednesday was my third congregation after all. My project was going to be a simple question.

What are these children learning about Church? Then all I needed was a method to determine the answer or answers to that question. I needed a spirit of invention to discuss these matters with the children, their parents, the volunteers, and the community representatives to compare the answers and make sense of them. I was a pastor who spent a lot of time drinking. I was not sure how I was going to get this done. First, though, I had to sell the project idea to the program advisor.

My academic program was in Biblical Interpretation and Proclamation. I spent a lifetime learning what interpreting the Bible was and how it was done through the two millennia of Christianity. No one seriously believes the idea where the text says what it means and means what it says. There are some interesting lists in the Bible, but it is not a book of lists. The whole process of finding out what a writer in the Bible is communicating to the original readers is merely one step in interpretation. A would-be interpreter should know a little information, in a lot of different disciplines of study. After all that work is done, the interpreter's job is to give a message that can be understood as being from Sacred Scripture as well as useful in the context of the interpreter. I have left out many steps and only touched lightly on some major points. The reader should know that for preachers to do their job right requires a very real commitment of time and brain power. My program advisor was going to be looking for this type of work in my project. I was going to have to convince him that I was doing the work described above in the context of a Children's Ministry. When I worked on my Master of Divinity degree, I received no instruction on working with children or children's ministry.

Courses in children's ministries were available. These classes were usually for people receiving a special certificate in the field of Christian Education. People to be ordained in The United Methodist Church were given a list of required courses to take in seminary. Classes in children's ministry, education, or even the pastoral care of children were not among them. It is really an oversight on our part as church leaders. John Wesley had several questions for early Methodist preachers. One of those questions is, "Will you teach the children in every place?" To this day, we answer in the affirmative to this question and wonder how we are supposed to do it. I am sure many clergy fulfill this vow in Confirmation class. Confirmation is perhaps the only time the children of the church have the attention of their pastor. The role of the pastor, as most people understand it, is to preach and visit the people who do not see many people other than their family members. These visits may take place in nursing homes, personal homes, or assisted living centers. Hospital visits are also very important in the life of the clergyperson. We often describe what we are doing as "being a spiritual presence" or "being a non-anxious caring presence." We talk about this part of our work as pastoral care. Essentially, it is merely acting in a way that demonstrates to the other person that someone gives a damn about them.

Hospital visits became my best pastoral care practice. I stood by the bedside of many people. I prayed with them. I held their hands. Yet, I did not cry with them. Why? There is something built into my psyche that allows me to delay my responses to crises. I often use humor in my visits.[1]

There have been occasions early in my service to churches where I met members of my church after they were admitted to the hospital. One lady became comfortable talking with me. She began to tell stories about her family. They were hilarious. I jumped into the conversation. We laughed, joked, and prayed. A week later she was comatose. I sat with her and her family as she was dying. One of her daughters looked up and said, "Momma said the high point of the week was when the preacher came to visit."

I do not like doing home or nursing home visits. They are often in cramped spaces. I get the impression that the patient was in a holding pattern waiting for someone from heaven to tell them it was time to land, and there were some very bizarre situations.

I had just left the room of one person who was rapidly failing. After talking a while and praying, I left her in the room surrounded by her family who were quietly saying their farewells while expressing their grief and love. As I was walking down the hallway to the elevator thinking about what a touching scene I was leaving behind, I heard a woman saying, "I knew you were in on this."

I looked over to her to see who she was talking to. It was me she was addressing. "I'm sorry," I said, "are you talking to me?"

"Yes," she replied forcefully.

I did not recognize this lady. She was wearing sunglasses and sitting in her wheelchair. I had no idea who she was. "Do you know me?" I asked.

Again, she replied in the affirmative.

"Do you remember my name?" She closed her eyes for a moment as though she were pondering. Then she said, "Yes. But I can't recall it now."

---

1. I recommend the book *House Calls* by Patch Adams, MD, for anyone interested in learning how to visit the sick.

I knew then that I had walked into an alternative universe. It was not the kind that one would think of in some science fiction story. No. This was a real alternative universe. Somehow through her dementia (which is my guess) she had a déjà vu experience. She saw me and thought she knew who I was and what I had done to her. I did not get too close to her. Experience had taught me that elderly people who suffer from cognitive problems can grab onto your wrist with one hell of a grip that you cannot get out of easily. I am always afraid of injuring the person.

This patient thought she had been abducted and abandoned at this place. I believe she thought I was one of the staff members. I told her I hoped she would feel better soon and left.

My mood darkened considerably after that. The end of one person's suffering did not end the suffering of that woman or any of the others like her. Suffering is something that never seems to end.

There is nothing pleasant about the suffering so many people experience when their lives are ending. My father once told me that I "get to tell people they are going to a better place." I do get to do that. Other times I get to be yelled at, scorned, and receive the blunt end of the frustration that various illnesses, including dementia, cause so many people. I can claim it is not fair to me, but it is not fair to them. It is a harsh reality I have a difficult time accepting.

When life gets depressing or a person suffers from clinical depression, he or she looks for a means of escaping reality. Using drugs or alcohol, is one way to do that. Other people go shopping, overeat, find someone to have sex with, and try to overcome the darkness with a little light. The problem remains. For many of us it is worsened by whatever it was we did to escape. My problems began to overflow into literally everything I did except drinking. All my work suffered while I suffered. My relationships were being corroded by everything happening to, within, and acted out by me.

My work suffered in many ways. So did my family life, and my academic work suffered as well. My escape was not working out too well. When I read the required books and essays, I read them and drank until the words blurred or made little sense. The alcohol-addled brain suffers even when the person is not drunk. Most social drinkers do not experience this phenomenon. They drink occasionally. Their drinking has a minimal effect on their health and their judgement in the long term. The alcoholic brain is affected in the long term. So is the rest of the body. I was vomiting, shaking, and sweating profusely. When I needed to make good decisions about important matters, I was too confused to make them.

My older son returned from his first year of college after being dismissed for academic reasons. He told me about it the morning after he returned home. I kept my cool. But later, when drinking, I came down hard on him. My younger son had an accident while driving in a parking lot near our home. I was drunk and shouted about how "stupid" he had been when he could have easily walked to the park. He went to bed that night with a terrible headache. I caused that.

Neither of my children are stupid. They are very bright, good, and loving people. From time to time, they screw up just like everyone else. To my mind at the time, their issues were out of proportion to the normal actions of other people. Who would those people be? Did I know anyone who fit the standard I was using? Of course not. Yet, I thought I was the normal person. I was the standard of proper behavior. It was addictive insanity.

Decisions about how to pay bills, how to get certain important jobs done, and how to allocate time were nearly impossible for me. Certain activities were easy because I had done them many times. Any new situation rendered me incapable. I was unstable and ready to explode in either rage or despair. It was a living hell for everyone in my family.

The hell was both in and from me. I resented everything and everyone. I made all the sacrifices to make everything possible for everyone. All everyone else in the house did was take from me. Of course, none of these claims were justified. It would take a long time to get my mind well enough to see how upside down all of this was to reality.

My mind was in trouble. My intellectual work suffered. It was nearly impossible for me to finish tasks. I had started a blog and let it drop. While I had a lot of information, I could not get it organized. I wrote trying to follow instructions. I proofread and edited as I thought I needed to do.

The doctoral program I was in required us to make three major appearances in Atlanta on the Emory University campus. Graduation was not included in that. I was involved in the January term (J-term). The intensive course we took was concerned with the Bible in Film. We watched fourteen different films.

I am a film junkie and thought it would be a sort of cakewalk course. I made some points during discussion that intrigued the professor. It was a week-long class. At one point, while leaving for lunch, the professor paid me a compliment.

"Do you write?" She asked me.

"Well, some." I replied. "I have a neglected blog; and I try my hand at science fiction from time to time."

"I was thinking if you didn't write we were all missing out."

I did not hear anything else the rest of the day. It gave me an ego boost. Such ego boosts are dangerous to an addict. People say alcoholics and other addicts are egomaniacs with severe inferiority complexes. It helped to offset something another professor had said at the end of the previous semester.

That professor said, "You have an A mind but only give a C effort." I was both angry and glad I did not have to deal with that person anymore. The other professor had paid a compliment that I used to justify myself. The J-term went well. The project was approved.

The day after I returned home, I told my wife what the J-term professor had said. She said, "Well, go to the den and get to writing." I did not, though. It was my day to relax from a long week before preaching the next Sunday. And I drank enough to make up for the days I had missed.

The following day I tried resurrecting the blog. But I could not think of a good topic to write about. My best efforts were still elusive. I could not do anything about it–anything that I really wanted to do, that is.

Chapter 3

My Life Destroyed

"YOU THOUGHT YOU WERE coming here to learn to drink responsibly." I cannot count how many times I heard those words during my twenty-eight days. Like a lot of sayings around recovery programs, you hear it until you are sick of it.

I already knew that twelve-step programs were abstinence-based programs. I learned that from the counselor I was going to before my stint in detox. The problem with any statement that begins "you thought . . ." is it is condescending and said with the intention to ridicule the person to whom it is said. I would experience more of this behavior before I was declared graduated from the treatment.

The intake process was my first indication something was wrong. My luggage was inspected. I was permitted to bring only literature of a spiritual nature. I was told to strip down to my underwear while my body and the clothes I wore were inspected. After dressing, I then sat with a counselor for a few hours while I answered a lot of questions. We had to stop for dinner before it could be finished. When that was over, the counselor asked me for my signature. He declared, "That's a great signature!" He continued. "Most patients are either too intoxicated or in withdrawal when they sign the forms." I thought it was an odd observation. My handwriting is terrible.

I was then sent to Nursing. There I was given tests for tuberculosis and alcohol. The nurse checked my weight, blood pressure, and discussed the medicines I brought with me. I was then given sheets and towels and taken to a room.

I was required to spend a couple of days in the medical detoxification unit. I did not understand this measure. I had detoxed at the beginning of the month. And then spent two weeks at home receiving an antibiotic for the staph infection I got in the hospital. I did not drink that whole time. The breathalyzer test showed no traces of alcohol. I thought that should be the end of it. It did not work that way. I was given a room to myself. It was not a private room per se, but there were no other patients in the room with me. There were two other beds in the room for when intake was busier.

I made the bed. The room was dark and unnecessarily cold. My suitcase was there. I had no contact with the outside world since my phone had been taken away. They kept my regular medication. I had to report to Nursing at a set time every morning. I unpacked my clothes and Bible which included the episcopalian Book of Common Prayer.

When I went to the men's common area, my fellow patients were barely conscious. The counselors on duty were not interested in us. They approached me only once to have my photo taken. It was meant to be the first picture in a "before and after" comparison. Since I arrived two weeks sober, I left looking the same.

Smoking breaks were allowed for us. I have never smoked. Yet, when I worked in the Marker Making room for Levi Strauss and Company, it was the only time I could socialize with my coworkers. I did the same in the detox facility. It was spring and the smoking area was the only place to sit outside. I sat among the smokers. We talked a lot about nothing. The topics were around booze and drugs and the number of different rehabs everyone else had been to. I was a rookie, the only one.

Mark was an older man. He was a lawyer who had a career in intoxication and rehabilitation that was unrivaled by the rest. Talking to him was fun when he was lucid. His voice was very mellow in tone. He spoke with deliberate precision.

"Don, how are you this morning?" He asked. He was enjoying his first smoke while I was drinking my first coffee.

"I am okay," I said. The fact was that I was depressed. I did not want to be there. I wondered why I was there. I wanted to get started just to be finished with it.

"That's good. Do you know what's for breakfast today?" he said.

"No, do you?"

"No. There is a menu on the door to the cafeteria, but sometimes it is wrong."

I was puzzled by this. "Well, we will know at 7:30.," I said finally. "There's always cereal." he said.

This was the most uninteresting conversation I ever had with anyone. He was more interesting to talk to later when he discussed his children and ex-wives. I was going to the newcomers group. He told me he would be in R and R. I replied I had heard there were a lot of railroad employees who would be there. He shook his head and said, "Relapse Recovery."

"Oh," was all I managed to say in reply. I wondered how "Relapse Recovery" worked differently than the program I would be joining. I could only guess it was more intensive. I was wrong about that, too.

When he left, I got to know my fellow newcomers. They were being weaned off the detox medications they were taking. Our conversations were predictably short. It was not until a counselor sent all the men to a meeting in one of the rooms that I started learning information about them. It was an introduction, so to speak, to a twelve-step meeting.

One railroad worker, Kyle, said, "Every time I've been to Narcotics Anonymous and A.A. meetings they sucked because of the 'thirteen steppers.'"

I did not hear anything else during that meeting until I finally asked, "What is that?"

The volunteer who was conducting our meeting explained, "It is where someone attends meetings—many different meetings—looking for a date." I liked how diplomatically he dealt with my ignorance.

I already knew that phenomenon well. Pastors know that there is a practice used by many middle-aged women and some men where a person will go from congregation to congregation looking for someone to date. This is a common enough practice in the Bible belt that everyone notices it. You hear some snide comments like, "Oh she is going there now? None of the single men here would have anything to do with her." It does not have a name. In recovery programs, they call it the thirteenth step because it is a way someone may use the meetings for something completely unrelated to the twelve-step program. I have since witnessed many thirteenth-step attempts at meetings.

Step thirteen is the reason male and female patients are kept separately in rehab centers. It is in this way, so it is believed, that unseemly bonding does not take place. I was assured in my time there that there was no truth in the rumors about babies being conceived at Cornerstone. I personally have my doubts. There were quite a few attempts at making romantic connections that I witnessed. The policy of separation is a good idea. Codependency is a major issue for many addicted persons.

When I was told I would be moving to the newcomer's area on the main campus, I packed up and put my bags in the hallway and then waited. And I waited. And I waited some more. I did not fully understand how "be ready by 3:30" translated into moving at 6:30. I am told that in the military "hurry up and wait" is the motto by which soldiers and sailors live. I believe in our case it was a matter of making sure everyone was getting their stuff together. Whether that meant patients or staff, I was not sure. It was likely both, and there was good reason for that.

I learned very quickly that most of the counselors were former patients of Cornerstone. This is a common practice in rehab. One of the administrative persons in the facility said it was because addicts and alcoholics were willing to work more cheaply than certified counselors and therapists. It is perversely logical. There is also another side to it that I will explain.

It began raining around 5 pm before we moved. The vehicles we were moved in were minivans. So, luggage and people, both males and females, were loaded up together to be moved. Yes, we got wet. When we arrived, the new building had a breezeway where we would be able to stay dry. I was glad for it. The weather in the latter part of April can prove to be warm and humid. Even with the rain, it was not any cooler than what we had experienced. The air conditioning in the minivan was not working. I was relieved to be doing something, though. The detox area was boring to say the least. There were television and videos. There was also the constant paperwork to fill out. The forms were mundane queries into how we felt, generally. The more interesting ones asked, "Are you experiencing any cravings," and "Are you having any drinking/using dreams?" The cravings question had a one through nine scale for us to indicate the severity. As to the second question, I was just starting to have dreams again, ones that did not include snakes or driving out-of-control vehicles. This brings me to the topic of feelings in general.

Putting it bluntly, for the recovering addict, feelings suck. I mean really and truly suck. By comparison, the withdrawal symptoms are mild. The recovering addict may die during withdrawal. When the feelings return you wish you had died.

The reason a person drinks or uses enough to become addicted is to shut off feelings. There is a psychic pain that all addicted people are trying to numb. There are many addicted people whose psychic pain comes from some sort of trauma. Some people may be self-medicating depression. Still others are experiencing so much negative stress in their lives that they use and drink, as it used to be said, "to forget." And that is part of the problem when a person is newly recovering. You remember.

You remember everything you have done and the effects that caused more problems in your life, work, and relationships. It is hard to describe how miserable you can feel. A person becomes morose, morbid, and despondent. The walls addicted people once placed around themselves are crumbling and falling inward. You want something or someone to make it all go away. You cannot sleep. The daily pain the addict attempted to numb returns after having waited for years. The feelings can be crushing.

Hindsight shows those feelings were being submerged in my quest for something or someone to take it away. I looked to God for that. I kept them locked deep inside of me until The Divine One decided to show up to receive them. It did not work out that way.

When we arrived at the inpatient center, where I would basically spend the remainder of twenty-eight days, I was greeted by a guy—a railroader from New York—who introduced himself as "The Mayor." The title was given to a patient who had been in the newcomer's program long enough to help everyone work into the system. I will call him Sam to protect his anonymity.

"Hey buddy," Sam began, "what's your name?"

I realized this was more than a merely friendly question. "Carlons," I said giving my first name. "But I go by Don."

He put out his hand. "Yes! You're with me."

I shook his hand. He led the way to our room. I had already received my room number and key card when we entered the first floor of the building. When we got to the door, he asked if I had my key card. I let go of my luggage and unlocked the door.

"They told you the key opens up the door downstairs, too?"

"Yep," I said trying to sound like I was comfortable in my surroundings. "I need it also to operate the elevator and to get into the building down the hill."

"They also want you to show it to the guys in the serving line for meals." He added.

I was given the bed next to the window. I started to unpack my stuff again. Sam interrupted me and told me I was on the list to go to a meeting that night. The van would be leaving soon. We would meet downstairs. Before we left, Sam wanted to show me the area I would be living in.

There were two common rooms. There was not supposed to be. A few adjustments to the living spaces between newcomers and relapse recovery gave the newcomer men two recreational rooms. These areas were equipped with coffee makers, refrigerators, cabinets for snacks (Don't leave anything there, I was warned.), television, and telephone. There were about three landlines for our area. We could use the phones at designated times. I really wanted to call home, but it was not a designated time. Besides that, I had to go downstairs to meet the van. I felt rushed.

I did not need my backpack, I was told. I readied myself to leave. I had my wallet with me. It was the first time I had it since going through intake. My cell phone was kept with some other contraband in an area I came to know as The Bullpen. Having my identification and money, I was feeling some sense of independence.

When we loaded up into the van, one guy looked at me and said, "Welcome to the druggy buggy." It was an odd but accurate term. The people who were being transported were alcoholics or addicts. We were taken in these unmarked white vans to meetings of either Alcoholics Anonymous or Narcotics Anonymous. The vans looked like rental passenger vehicles from the nearby airport. They were plain white metal boxes on four wheels. If we went to meetings, to see a doctor, or to the other Cornerstone campus, it would be in one of these vans.

Before I was taken to the newcomer area, I was given a ring binder with worksheets in them including one called "The First Step." In addition to that, I received paperback editions of the Alcoholics Anonymous "big book" and the Narcotics Anonymous Basic Text, which is like the former book except for material on drug addiction, updated language, and different testimony stories in the back. Just about everything in the first one hundred sixty-four pages in the A.A. big book is also in Narcotics Anonymous with some tweaking of the text here and there. I was given a few pens, too.

My first recovery group meeting was in a United Methodist Church building I was familiar with once. The thought occurred to me that I might see someone I knew there. Worse yet, I might see someone that knew me. I only wanted this stuff to be done quickly and quietly. Of course, all I had to do was look through a window and see that there was someone there that I knew. He was one of my colleagues too. I cursed my luck with a rhyming word. There was nothing to do except go in and sit down some-where among the tables.

The guy I recognized was handing out some literature to us he passed by me and quietly said, "You look like a Methodist preacher I know." He went on about his task. What I feared happened. Someone recognized me.

I soon let that thought go. The other men who came to the meeting with me were helpful. I got some coffee. I listened while the meeting began with the Serenity Prayer and the readings. The meeting was like some adult Bible studies I held in special seasons. Then the question came, "Is there anyone here who has never been to a recovery meeting before?"

I raised my hand.

"Would you tell us your name and where you are from?" The chair-person asked me.

I heard myself say the words, "My name is Don." Most of the other patients had not met me yet. "And I am an alcoholic," I added. These words summed up my identity and how I was regarded. I listened to the testimo-nials some of the others gave. At one point, I told the story of my recent experiences. It was another step in my introduction to the other newcom-ers. At the end of the meeting came, we were told about the chip system. It is a color-coded calendar of days one has been sober. There is a white starting chip. And the other colored chips represented quantities of days without drinking. They were in increments of thirty days, sixty days, ninety days, and then a chip for six months, and another for nine months. To my count, I had seventeen days including the time in the hospital and home recovering from a staph infection. I took the white chip with everyone of-fering congratulatory applause. The meeting ended with everyone circling up and saying the Lord's Prayer together. I lingered a little while to talk to my colleague Hal.

"I am gonna hug your neck," he said. This is a local expression show-ing how proud one is of the other person. I told Hal I was just starting at Cornerstone. I would likely see him again. I reflected later, on the irony of how I never knew he was in recovery, and how he did not know I needed help. Not that there was anything he could have done to help. I know my ego would have gotten in the way. I went into that meeting not wanting to be recognized by anyone at all. I was relieved that it happened anyway.

The next day began my routine.

I was warned at intake that the daily routine would be busy and in-tense. I did not find it that way. To me it was boring, very boring. Often it was mind-numbingly boring. I was not the only one who felt that way about it. The reprieve from boredom came at mealtime and fitness times.

Each morning we would be awakened by a knock on the door from the night counselor. We would get ready for the day and sit in the common room drinking coffee and waiting until the nurse opened the "Medpass," which was a small closet space where everyone's daily medications were passed out. Usually, the lines were long because the Relapse Recovery men came down to the same Medpass. It was open three times per day.

We would carry the day's literature in our backpacks down to breakfast. From there we went to "Morning Spiritual." During that time, a chaplain would walk us through the daily readings of three different devotional books, have us answer the daily question. The answers began with "Today, I will . . ." The end task of the half-hour would be handing out the daily packet. The daily packet contained several pages stapled together that detailed which subgroups would be at different times of the day. They were designated as groups A, B, and C. Railroad workers would be another subgroup. Airline pilots were another group. At times, the "Professionals" group was called to a special meeting. The professionals were from those jobs that required a state-issued license or state board supervision. There were times where a person found himself in more than one subgroup.

Another subgroup was what type of therapy a person was to receive. I was placed in Cognitive Behavioral Therapy (CBT). For the most part, these designations made perfect sense. During our time in the detox area, our intake questionnaires were evaluated. This evaluation was used by the therapy staff to determine where we were sent. Like I said, it made perfect sense. But the system relied on a person self-reporting. Often a person was more concerned with how they would be perceived. A clever person could use the opportunity to lie about their circumstances to hide any criminal activity. People in denial about past childhood trauma, for instance, would put themselves in the wrong group.

The usual weekday had us in therapy of some sort. There was one called "relapse prevention." Another group involved sitting with our counselor listening to another person explain what he learned from his homework packet. These packets included emotional and mental health topics. I am pretty good at reading comprehension. I assumed it would be easy until I had to do it.

"What are you doing?" one guy asked.

I looked at our counselor. She stared back. "I am giving what I read." I said finally.

"I know. You are not here to give a book report," he said.

"What?" I asked, confused by what he said.

"Tell us what the packet means to you. Don't just say what you read from it." he said.

I was shocked. I had missed the point. The guy who called me out was a younger fellow. He was also a veteran of rehabs. The only reason he was designated a newcomer was because his relapse had been too soon for him to be classified for R.R. He knew what the counselor expected to hear from us.

We were supposed to testify. The counselor gave each of us packets of reading material based on the evaluation made from the entry papers. Essentially, we were receiving a diagnosis. Our task was to see our symptoms for ourselves. If I received a packet on low self-esteem, my job then was to tell how I identified with the issue. I was not supposed to tell what it was to have Low Self Esteem. I was to describe how bad my self-esteem was. In other words, our task was to be convinced. We had to accept the diagnosis. Somehow by doing so, we could explain our addictive behaviors.

The next time I had to report on one of my other packets, the therapist showed up and sat in on the meeting. But this time a leading counselor sat in too. The topic had to do with trauma.

Once I gave my report the leading counselor asked me what I wanted now.

"I don't want to have to go on medical leave. I want to go back and do my job and be with my family."

"You can do that," she began. "Look at all you have accomplished and overcome so far. And you are a minister. You help other people with their problems."

"Not really," I said. "No one ever gets better."

"You can do this," she said.

I just want to get this crap over with, I thought. There was more. I was being singled out. The main reason was that I was being more than just passive aggressive with the staff. I was downright belligerent. Sometimes, I did it without intending to do so.

My cognitive behavioral therapy class leader was the prime example of an inmate running the asylum. We spent too many hours listening to his testimonials. He had been to treatment twice at Cornerstone. "Do you think I wanted that," was his typical whine.

One idea that has stuck with me for many years is that the whiners got exactly what they wanted, only to complain about it. Attention is the thing whiners want more than anything else. It is a sickness that does nothing other than annoy me. It is almost a trigger for me. My response to it—sometimes out loud—is, "The hell you didn't." This time I attempted to keep my cool and count the days, but people like him are determined to make it difficult.

I suffered some sinus issues during the midpoint of the time I was there. I was almost always wanting something hot to drink to help with the congestion. Coffee was usually available in the dining area. There were times, though, when the floors were being mopped or for some other reason the portable barrier was put up. All of us, including staff members, ignored it. As the old saying goes, it is not illegal until you get caught.

One of the directors caught me, "What are you doing back there?"

"Getting coffee before my next class," I replied.

"You are not supposed to be back there when this," he indicated the barrier, "is out."

"The 'Caution Wet Floor' sign isn't out," I said, confused by his objection.

"You are not supposed to be there at all when the barrier is pulled out," he said and went upstairs.

I shrugged and watched another person go behind the barrier only to find the coffee pots were empty.

One afternoon, I filled my travel mug full of coffee. The CBT whiner came in to begin class and told us not to have drinks in the class. I quickly opened the spout on my mug to drink from it before putting it on the floor beside the wall. The cap made a loud clicking noise. It was noticed.

The whiner looked at me. "I am serious. You are not supposed to have that in here."

"I just needed some . . ."

"I said, you can't have it here."

I got up to put the cup next to the wall away from the table where I sat.

"You should pour it out," he said.

I sat my cup on the floor and explained, "We are not supposed to be in the halls during the hour." I sat down.

Later, at supper, one of the airline guys said, "Don, you are my hero."

I replied, "I did not mean to be defiant. It merely looked that way."

"Sure," he said. His wink indicated he did not believe me.

The next day, predictably so, my therapist came and said, "We need to talk." It was my second trip to the office. My therapist asked me to wait outside while he went in to talk to someone else. While I was there, the CBT guy opened his office door and started to leave. Seeing me out there, he looked distressed and quickly shut himself in his office. I knew then why I had been called. This time I was in front of the director who caught me getting coffee from the dining room.

The director told me what he had been told by the whiner.

I explained why I had the coffee to begin with. Then I told him I was not being *entirely* defiant because it wasn't my intention to do so. My therapist said, "In Don's defense, he has had sinus issues for a while now," and that was the end of it.

Drug and alcohol treatment centers do little in the way of treatment beyond that of medical detoxification and having a patient talk to a psychiatrist or a psychologist. I spoke to a psychiatrist once in the whole month. He diagnosed me, again from a self-reporting worksheet, as having severe depression. This much I already knew. I had been taking an antidepressant for fifteen years previously. The doctor explained antidepressants usually do not help beyond five years. That explained why I felt like a did. He prescribed a different one for me. This was the only time my medication was changed or discussed while I was at Cornerstone.

I only lodged one complaint about a staff member while I was there. Few of the people on staff were truly qualified to work in their field. Hiring addicts and alcoholics in recovery saved money in salaries. It also brought the worst people for the job of offering care, and created a cultish atmosphere.

One staff member was standing in for the regular person in the group. He was abusive. This guy exploded on the group.

"I don't get nothing out of doing this but a paycheck! That's all you all are to me. I leave here and go home every night and don't give a damn about you anymore." The rest of the discussion was more of the same. He may have been frustrated that he had to cover for someone else. I don't know. Everyone in the group was angry.

The next morning, I reported it to the counselor. Some of my fellow patients stormed out at that point not wishing to discuss it. I wondered if they were angry with me. No one said anything about it to me.

It was Saturday. Everyone needed a break. We were taken to an off-campus meeting where that staff member showed up and spewed on the group at the meeting. A week later I was back in the office for something I said.

"What is being done about T?" I asked.

"We've decided to just let that go and move on." I was told. I almost asked why we did not just "move on" from anything I said or did. The message, however, was clear. The patients were open to abuse. We were not really patients. We were more like asylum inmates. And we would be held accountable. Staff could do what they wanted with us. I never trusted any of them again.

Sundays were family visitation days. My family was a little over an hour's drive away from me. I filled out the necessary paperwork for my wife and both sons to visit for a few hours Sunday afternoons. I called each Wednesday night prior to the visit to ask if they would come. I was told my oldest son, Philip, would likely be working on Sunday. He usually did work on Sunday mornings. Just in case though, I filed a visitor request for him too.

My wife was the only one who came. I had not seen her for two weeks. I missed them. "I guess Philip had to work," I began. "Where's Sean?"

"He is hanging out with friends," she said.

My wife brought some candy bars and other supplies I had asked for. We presented them for inspection and then went to find a place where we could visit. We were not allowed in the residential area or the common rooms there.

The railroaders came from states all over the country. If their families were going to be there at all it would be during the "family fundamentals" weekend. It was the time members of the immediate family or household would come for group meetings with family members of other patients. Some would be able to afford the trip. Others could not. There were those spouses who would not come to the therapy.

Divorce papers arrived for some patients. I suppose we were in the best place to be for that kind of news. There was nothing then to do but be resigned to being in the facility. Medical help was available. Emotional help was there too. I considered myself immune. And then I started seeing the cracks.

My sons never came to see me. My father came once. But he did not stay long since he thought he was interfering with my wife's visit that day. It was all right. I needed to talk to her.

I called her the night I was told to which "Family Fundamentals" weekend I was assigned. Immediately, she said she could not come. The program required all day on Friday and Saturday with a half day on Sunday. Being a high school teacher, she would need to get a substitute for Friday. "I won't be able to get a sub then," she said.

I did not understand that. I called to give her a couple of weeks' advance notice because I knew she would have to get someone to cover for her. When I asked why she was not even bothering to try, her response was it was the end of the school year.

I checked with the counselors. They assured me that we could come as a family to a Family Fundamentals weekend any time within the year. I supposed it was a policy made for such occasions.

"We'll see," is all she said when I told her. I realized she did not intend to make any effort to take part.

She talked a lot about her students. She coached the women's soccer team. She spoke often about them. One girl she mentioned was dating a guy of which she did not approve.

"Why?" I asked.

"Because he hangs out with drug addicts."

"Who do you think I am hanging out with here?" I asked in reply.

"I am not sure I want to hang out with you anymore," she said.

I thought she was kidding. It was only later when I realized she was not joking. I went to Family Fundamentals and listened to what the family members of other patients experienced while their loved one was in active addiction. It was the first time I experienced a craving for alcohol during the time I was inpatient.

Family Fundamentals was one of the few times male and female patients were together. My heart went out to one woman whose husband played the martyr. This was one reason male and female patients were normally kept apart. It was too easy to become empathetic with someone in group meetings that you could become attracted to and romantically involved with them. I wondered how my wife would have behaved if she had come.

Physical pain from what I later learned was from inflammatory joint disease and esophagitis began plaguing me. I wound up going to the emergency room at the local hospital when I experienced a lot of pain in my chest. I asked the nurse if I could make a call home. When I called, my wife told me Cornerstone had contacted her already.

I asked her if she was coming down. She was working on a master's degree at the time. She said she was too busy. I was upset about it. The ER doctor decided it was arthritis related and ordered Toradol. I felt better for about three days after that.

The day for me to leave was nearing. A counselor came over and sat across from me during lunch to ask about my reported cravings. "During Family Fundamentals we stopped using euphemistic terms such as 'active addiction' and talked about vodka and wine that way." She agreed that must have been the reason. It was not brought up again.

The final day was a Friday, and it was eventful. Basically, everything was being done the same way. For me though, I was ready to leave. Then the senior counselor came to me.

"Don," she began, "someone named Jim Tallent called and wants a conference call with us."

A familiar stressor had arrived. No other employer would dare try to have a medical consultation over an employee's condition. Churches expect to know everything. Unfortunately, church hierarchies often include very insecure people. Jim was one of the worst.

"He is my district superintendent," I said. "My boss," I added.

"We have to have your permission to talk to him," she replied.

Later, we gathered in the therapist's office. The senior counselor was there as well. I thought I had better explain something.

"All Jim is looking for are assurances. I know you can't fully assure him. But he will try every scenario to get them from you." I told them.

The call was made. The superintendent began talking and asking questions. The staff members were wide-eyed with disbelief. We answered his questions. During the conversation, the therapist talked about my progress and made recommendations that they made for everybody.

"We believe Don would be helped by taking part in an intensive outpatient program." Intensive Outpatient (IOP) required me to do the same thing all over again for two months while driving over an hour each way four days a week. This time would be added to my time on the job and the time I would need in trying to patch things up at home.

"That is optional?" I asked.

The superintendent chimed in. "Well, if your therapy team thinks it is in your best interest, I believe you should."

"Are there any programs closer to home for me?" I asked the team.

"We think so." It turned out to be untrue.

Basically, the conversation ended there. Then Jim began the what if questions. They reminded me of the scenarios he asked about when I was home with the IV bag. I lightly kicked the senior counselor's foot. She nodded and shook her head in disbelief.

We eventually got through the superintendent's concerns. I started calling the potential IOPs. It was to no avail. Being Friday afternoon, it was not surprising. I then sat down with my regular counselor and made an Aftercare Plan. It included a pledge not to drink, to read a daily recovery related devotional, and go to ninety meetings in ninety days unless I was doing IOP. It was the last hoop before "coining out."

Coining out is a ceremony for having finished the program. The departing patient receives a medallion which is the size of a coin. After that, the patient listens while fellow patients and the counselor for your sub-group tell about their hopes for the person and something about how far one has come in getting better.

I could not sleep that night. I was too excited to be going home. My wife and Sean arrived. Since it was Saturday, I had to hunt for a senior staff member to inspect my room and sign me out. That took a little time. And I was impatient. When it was done. She drove home.

"Do you want to stop by Firehouse?" she asked.

"No, let's just go home. I am tired."

When we got home, my wife announced that she had work to do and shut herself up in her workroom. Sean went upstairs to his room. I shrugged it off. I unpacked and started my laundry. There had been an issue with bedbugs in one of the rooms at Cornerstone. Thankfully, it was not mine nor was that room adjacent to my room. But I was not taking any chances.

Essentially, I was home alone. I went to the bedroom and took a nap.

When I woke up, I went downstairs to work on the laundry. I knocked on the door to my wife's workroom and asked if she wanted all of us to go out to eat. She said she was too busy. I was disappointed. A month had gone by. I was not getting any sort of welcome home.

I drove to the liquor store and bought a bottle of brandy and one of wine. I drank heavily for three days. Two weeks later, I began IOP, my marriage ended, and I drank again. I informed the district superintendent and our insurance person. I was taken into the Sober Living Facility at Cornerstone and placed on voluntary medical leave by the church.

Chapter 4

God and Treatment

I TOOK A COMBINATION Bible and Book of Common Prayer with me to Cornerstone. Sometimes I even read it. I always had good intentions. Time would get away from me. I remember one evening reading the Letter of James and thinking about what I could have done with the time I spent drinking. I was ashamed of myself, but God was going to be a major issue for me.

One morning I sat outside the dining room near the outdoor tables and read Morning Prayer II. I was just past the scripture readings when a group of new newcomers brought their breakfast trays outside. One patient, John, asked what I was doing.

"I am reading the morning devotions," I said.

"Do you have a reading to share with us?" John asked.

"Well," I began to say I just passed those but changed my mind and turned back to the Gospel reading. It was the story of how Jesus calmed the storm on the Sea of Galilee.

When I finished the reading, I automatically said, "The word of God for the people or God. Thanks be to God."

The guys at the table replied together, "Thanks be to God." One fellow, a pilot added, "Thanks be to Don . . . for reading it."

John then asked. "How do you interpret that story?"

"I don't interpret it. Right now, I just meditate on it." Then I remembered something my New Testament professor had said. "One thing I do know," I began, "is the word for 'rebuked' as in "he rebuked the storm," is the same for when Jesus rebukes demons."

John nodded. We all got back to what we were doing.

Since I was never going to get away from the God question, I would never get away from my vocation. One of the railroad guys always referred to me when he introduced new patients to us as "the goddamned minister." On another occasion, a fellow I had not met previously was telling me he heard there was a priest in the group.

"He's not really a priest," I said. "He's a Protestant minister."

He thought a moment and looked back over to me. "It's you, isn't it?" he said finally.

"Yes."

There were also guys who told me they were atheists. One fellow had a difficult time with my sense of humor. "God damn it, Don!" He would say in frustration. I always replied, "Who damn it?"

There were also serious issues with the discussion of God. One young guy voiced his frustration to me. "I just don't get the God thing," he said.

"You don't have to," I said. "You can ask for literature that is more in line with your thinking."

He checked into it and returned. "Thanks Don. I didn't know they had this." Then he asked, "Why would you help me get information because I don't believe?"

I shrugged. "The goal here is to get better. I think we should help each other get what we need," I said.

"I like you, Don," he said. That statement was gratifying. It was nice to know I helped him. My body was dealing with the new antidepressants, so I did not feel any better about it. I simply did what I do. I began to think that was the whole problem.

I have always doubted my calling. Perhaps, I should not have ever gone into ministry. I even struggle with having faith in God. And I knew I was going to have to struggle harder with these questions of faith and vocation while I was in treatment.

There were people on staff and contracted with the facility who were called chaplains or spiritual advisors. There were also some good volunteers. Jeff, my colleague I called on while I was in the hospital was one of those volunteers. In fact, there was another United Methodist Licensed Pastor working there. He was the chaplain for our group during Morning Spiritual.

I recognized him right off. Later, I spoke with him in the hallway.

"Where are you serving now?" I asked.

"Williamson Chapel," he said.

"You know, I was there for a while."

"I know."

"So, you know who I am then." I was not certain because I had not served in the local area for a long time.

He said, "Yeah. I just thought it would be better if you approached me. I didn't want to put you on the spot."

"I see," I said. Then we fell into talking about the Williamson Chapel Church.

I am still astonished by how I became the pastor for Williamson Chapel. In October of 1996, I received a telephone call from the Maryville District Superintendent. His name was Bob Bostick. Previously, I had met with him about how I could enter the United Methodist Church with my Church of Christ credentials.

"I need someone to preach at one of our local churches," he said.

"This Sunday?" I asked.

"This Sunday until June," he replied.

"Oh," I said. "Where is it located?"

"I don't know," he said. He was new to the area and the job. "Its name is Williamson Chapel."

I was silent.

"Are you familiar with it?" he asked.

"Yeah, that is where my maternal grandparents and great-grandparents are buried."

I think he was surprised to learn that. "So, you will do it?"

"Let me think about it," I said.

I talked to my wife about it. Our son Philip was only six months old. Eventually we decided that they would attend Alcoa First United Methodist Church while I drove to Williamson Chapel on Sundays. We only had one car at the time. The schedule worked out well. "Until June" turned out to be June of 1999. Then I became a full-time student appointee of the Holston Conference.

The coincidence of my connection to that church and being the one sent there during a crisis fuels the kind of story evangelical Christians like to tell as an example of Divine Providence. The Bible includes stories like that. God provides for Elijah thru his trials, for instance. Jacob's sheep breed in ways that benefit him. These are stories of divine action of provision for the faithful. It is easy to fall into patterns of thinking based on the idea that God will take care of us. The only problem is for a sensitive person to see that Divine Providence does not appear to work in the lives of other people. If we ever fall into the trap of saying a tragedy, the death of a child, or a natural disaster, is God's will or an act of providence, we are essentially claiming to worship a moral monster. Why does God's providence work for some and not others? It can easily be claimed that being faithful brings rewards. The Bible never claims that faithfulness on the part of the believer is a one hundred percent guarantee. The epic Job makes that clear. Do we really think the Creator of the Universe is contractually bound to give us what we want? If all the things that ever happened to me in my life were God's will, then it is God's will that I nearly drank myself to death. That is a truly insane thought.

The utterly ridiculous notion of reward for faithfulness allows pastors to give assurances to congregants who, if they believe it, must then make up excuses for why God has not rewarded them. This idea too makes God into a caricature of evil.

Bill W. and Dr. Bob laid out the twelve steps that allow "God as we understand Him." The phrase "Higher Power" is also used in twelve step programs. To many Christians, these phrases about God are unacceptable.

Churches have come up with alternative programs for recovering addicts and alcoholics. *Celebrate Recovery* is the best example of these types of efforts. Having begun at Rick Warren's Saddleback Church in California, *Celebrate Recovery* has been marketed to evangelical and mainline churches as a Christian approach to recovery. The program is even marketed to individual persons through educational materials including an edition of the Bible complete with notes and testimonials that are designed to aid in recovery.

A Buddhist version of the twelve-step approach called *Refuge Recovery* was marketed by Noah Levine. However, the program became mired in scandal and has been halted in many places. Another version of the idea, *Recovery Dharma*, deliberately separated from Levine, has been marketed as well.

The idea of "God as we understand him" has become such a stumbling block for many. It is not uncommon to hear someone define their understanding of the Divine One as being defined in the Bible. Other people have claimed they did not get well until they found their connections to God through Jesus. While these views are perfectly acceptable in most recovery programs, it is not an official position of the program. A sponsor should not attempt to convert someone they sponsor to any theological idea.

I remember my friend who visited me in the hospital told me that in practice there were two kinds of *Celebrate Recovery*. One way was about "deliverance from addiction." This is the belief that addiction is a demonic activity in someone's life. Casting out a demon is involved in attempting to heal from addiction. The second way was to follow the program without any added ideas from differing denominations. Human nature being what it is, AA and NA also have those who attempt to control another person's belief system "for their own good."

The question remains, "Do we need a power greater than ourselves to help us overcome our addictions?" Probably not. However, we do need some sense of accountability in our lives to keep us from drinking or using. God can become a useful tool in the process of overcoming addiction. For a person to claim, "God loves me," or "My Higher Power wants to make my life better without drinking or using" is to seek some sort of accountability.

It is not correct, though, to say a Higher Power is merely a crutch. A crutch is designed to keep a person standing. The most important attribute concerning God for the addicted person is that God picks up people after they fall. The basic assumption of the twelve-step program is that some Higher Power helps bring about and maintain a person's sobriety. The only thing an individual addict must do to begin the process of overcoming their addiction is to confess.

Conversion in the Abrahamic faiths are done either by confession or profession or both. The twelve-step approach originated among people whose spiritual life was shaped by Christianity. It is not surprising then that people must first confess their major sin. "We admitted we were power-less over alcohol—our lives have become unmanageable," is how the first step reads. The second is this, "(We) Came to believe that a Power greater than ourselves could restore us to sanity." The issue is not whether addicted people can stop on their own. The fact is most people can stop drinking or using for a time unless they need medical help with detoxing. The question is, "can these people remain abstinent on their own?" This question does not touch the issue raised by some who have settled into "moderate" drinking. AA and NA along with *Rational Recovery* and *Recovery Dharma* all maintain that an addicted person must remain abstinent. "To drink is to die"[1] reminds a person to maintain abstinence. And the gray area of the solution to addiction appears again. How can we say some person is addicted? Churches, law enforcement, and media have promoted in some way or another the concept of "one drink, drunk" or "one hit, hooked." These claims are made to inflate the dangers involved. The actual dangers should be stressed. Ridiculous claims do not help anyone.

I recall the first time I went to a Cornerstone group meeting while in treatment that was called a First Step meeting. The purpose of the meeting was confession. The meeting was about people admitting their powerlessness over a substance and the unmanageability of their lives. When we were sent from the detox area to the residential one, we were given twelve-step literature and the ring binder that included First Step paperwork. The questionnaire was intended to lead a patient to the point.[2]

The questions reminded me of tests I took in middle school. The person who was doing his First Step in front of the group read his answers to each question. The composition of the group was a counselor (of any gender) and the peers of the patient (same gender). It did not matter that some of the group members selected by the staff had yet to do the First Step. After the patient gave his answers, the peer group were told to bow their heads, close their eyes, and only answer the prepared questions the counselor gave by raising their hand to give an affirmative answer. One question the counselors asked was, "Does he appear to accept the disease model of addiction?" There is nothing on the questionnaire about that topic. This fact bothered me. But I always answered that the patient accepted the idea. Why? Because I knew the staff would double-down on a person who they believed did not get that idea.

When I entered Cornerstone, and for some time afterward, I accepted addiction was a disease. Presently, the Diagnostic and Statistical Manual of Mental Disorders, 5th Edition (DSM-V) calls my form of addiction "Alcohol Abuse Disorder." In other words, I do not have "alcoholism" even though I can be called an "alcoholic." Members in recovery groups often refer to their condition as a "progressive disease." You hear statements like "my disease" as though it is a person. For example, "While I am in these rooms, my disease in the parking lot doing pushups," or "My disease has been speaking to me." Addiction is indeed a mental health issue. But no other disease is ever personified by its victims this way unless they see it in religious terms.

1. *Alcoholics Anonymous*, 66.
2. You can read the quiz in Appendix A.

The idea that addiction is a demonic entity that must be rebuked, cast out, and healed from fits in very nicely with a religious framework. We can pray for someone to be cured of cancer. And patients can talk about their cancer as an enemy. The oncologist though does not see cancer in this way.

Addicted people become so because the pleasure/reward system of the brain is stimulated by the drug of choice. They become addicted because of continued stimulation of this system by using the substance as opposed to any other stimulus. If the situation is out of control, the addict neglects everything else in life to continue receiving the stimulation the substance provides. Despite claims made in popular media, no addiction gene has been found.[3] Indeed, no physical causation has been discovered for addiction. There are ways to medically treat dependency and the dangerous withdrawal symptoms. Once a patient is medically stabilized, then work on the other areas of the person's life can begin. However, that does not justify the thirty to ninety days of incarceration that happens in rehab.

What does any of this have to do with God of one's own understanding? As I said above, it is about accountability. The best way to understand alcohol abuse is that it is a behavior. And behaviors can be linked to a person's perspective on life, personal background, and other mental and emotional health issues. My addiction has been based on all three of the links just given. My perspective on life is that of difficulty and no rewards for taking the correct actions in life. My personal background included a childhood of constant criticism, and always being told I was not good enough. I also suffer from clinical depression and have emotional issues from the trauma that was just described. Searching for an addiction gene leaves out the need for repairing the person. The sense of helplessness that instruments like the questionnaire imposes on those who answer it keeps that repair from happening. The addicted person is encouraged to think of himself as being irreparable unless his own image of God does the work.

Accountability means the exact opposite. This is what twelve-step programs get right. Addicted people are encouraged to look clearly at their own faults and to understand that they cannot alter the behaviors and faults of others, they can then choose to do what is needed to restore relationships, get his or her life into some sort of manageability, and get professional help to change their behavior toward more constructive actions. It works only if a person is willing to be held accountable. Something I was not willing to do.

3. Dodes and Dodes, *Sober Truth*, 88–89.

My mother accused me one time saying, "You don't like discipline." It was true. Her understanding of discipline and mine were basically the idea of discipline as punishment. If a parent had an unruly child, it was because the parent failed to discipline the child. If children are effectively punished (and this often means inflicting pain), then they will learn the boundaries of their behavior. The familiar quote "Spare the rod and spoil the child" is often considered to be Holy Scripture. It was written by Samuel Butler. My mother was beaten as a child. I was beaten as a child, teenager, and young adult. I was rebellious. As a small child, I was subjected to religious abuse by being told that the Bible said I should be stoned to death for disobedience (this was from the associate minister's wife). And I was told that if I did not do everything God's way, I would spend eternity in hell. I have no use for the God of their understanding. Continuous threats and criticism plagued me constantly during what I was told were the best years of my life. When I became an adult, I feared every time I had to go to a performance review.

The church attracts some people who only understand accountability as judgmentalism. While these are not the only people in churches, they are the most vocal. Their hypocrisy becomes all too evident. The criticisms they lay on their clergy leaders are inexcusable. Denominational leaders who allow it to happen to "keep the peace" are just as guilty. I have heard from many people in recovery groups that they simply cannot stand being around such people. They see the churches as being full of hypocrites because there is often no one who will hold such people accountable for their actions. It is impossible to remain sane and accept the God of their understanding, too.

My attempt in ministry was to proclaim a God that was different from the abusive and judgmental divinity that these people obviously believed supported their own spitefulness. It continues to be that way. Yet, I react strangely to it because I worked myself into a way of being that pushes me toward self-destruction. I have had my share of constructive criticism but was unable to recognize it as being positive. It is too easily confused with the unfair kind. I have heard rejection after rejection when I would not simply tell people what they wanted to hear. Lay people who believe they are righteous in their thoughts and ways have accused me of trying to get them to learn something or, worse yet, to think. I have not been trying to get them to intellectualize their lives. I simply wanted them to consider what they said and did to other people. And through all of it, God has been silent. I began to drink more and more to drown out the other voices. There was one other voice I did not care to hear anymore too.

I believed deep down the unfair criticism was true. You are not good enough, I said. I could point out the good things I did. But I heard the voice say, "you want gratitude? Were those things done for gratitude and praise? You do not deserve them." As a child, I never believed I deserved happiness. I could not feel like I ever got it. As an adult I believed if I rested, I was being lazy. If I did anything, I should feel guilty. And if I expected appreciation, it was hubris. When someone said I was doing a good job, I could not accept the compliment. I heard I was spiritual. I only felt like I was knowledgeable about spiritual things. When my wife tried to say I was a good person, I still could not believe I was loved.

I knew I did good things for people. I knew I worked hard. I knew I tried my best. I also believed it was never good enough. I wanted more than anything to walk away from life and never be seen again. Still, I hoped someone would miss me. I was full of self-pity. But I was also suffering from stress, anxiety, and depression. I could not separate the self-pity from the other three. I could not say where they fit together. Most of all, I had doubts about everything.

When I got home from inpatient treatment, all those things came rushing back into my mind. The twenty-eight-day experience did not give me new insights. If it did anything, it helped me know what I resented the most in my life. When I got home, I poured my resentments about our life together out on my wife. None of these problems were her fault. She was as she was. You cannot blame the sun for rising and setting as it does. It is, after all, the earth that is moving. I was trying to earn what should have been freely given. The brokenness of my toxic life never let me see if it ever was given.

She suggested we separate. Later when I asked her what she was going to do, her words stung, "I will stay for right now" I said. "No." I felt like I was hearing "to see if you screw up again." It was the day before her birthday. The next day I went to IOP and before returning home I bought her a small birthday cake so she and our sons could celebrate. I also bought a small bottle of brandy and drank it empty while sitting in the den away from them. She found me passed out in the chair. She poured out what was left in my glass, put a blanket over me, and turned off the light.

I had another meeting with my district superintendent the next day. I was sick from the booze. I could only drink coffee at what was supposed to be a lunch meeting. I attended a recovery meeting that morning. I said nothing about drinking the night before.

The superintendent was leaving that job in a few weeks to be senior pastor at a church where they had a *Celebrate Recovery* program and where a few Cornerstone administrators attended. He was concerned that on social media I said I was giving up theology as a discipline and was opting for philosophy instead. I explained that there was merely a difference in approach involved.

"But your churches looked to you as the resident theologian," he said.

"I think they look to me as someone who is supposed to teach and preach what I understand from Scripture."

Then he got to his concern, "I want to make sure you are preaching Jesus and not Big Book."

I held my outrage in place. Here was the very person who forced me into the treatment center and IOP, and now his insecurities allowed him to say something so unbelievably stupid to me.

I replied, "You know that my area of study for my doctorate is 'Biblical Interpretation and Proclamation' don't you?"

"Actually, I did not know that," he said. That was not surprising as a friend pointed out to me that Jim was entirely focused on maintaining the institution. My addiction and recovery threatened that.

"You don't have anything to worry about in that way." I assured him.

He told me what would be done if I relapsed, and then the meeting was over. I was disturbed by everything going on at the time. My wife did not want to go to counseling. I was having trouble. And so, I decided to quit.

I called Jim later and told him I already had relapsed. He thanked me for my honesty. I also told him Cornerstone was now requiring me to go to their Sober Living Facility (SLF) or else I would be expelled from IOP. It was going to cost me eight hundred dollars per month for two months. I had room on a credit card. Jim asked me to call the Pastor-Parish Committee chair. Later he called me back. The bishop said I should go on voluntary medical leave. I would receive seventy-five percent of my salary as a stipend for the next appointment period.

I drove myself back to the detox center at Cornerstone the next morning. I was miserable. I was no longer trying to save a job or a marriage. I was looking for an escape. I did not know where else to go. I had failed at everything.

Stan, my IOP counselor, was the best at what he did during my two stays. He came to see me in the detox area. "I don't see you as a failure," he said. "You have made it back." I did not know what to make of that statement. I saw returning as failure. I decided to trust Stan though. You could tell that he cared if we lived or died. I knew his words were sincere. I then began to understand accountability in recovery.

Chapter 5

The Faith Struggle

BEING A PERSON OF faith, it is hard to maintain faith—in anything. It is a paradox. Many times, both as a child and as an adult, I asked about the whole salvation problem. Let me sum it up in this fanciful dialogue.

Me: Why was I born to go to hell?

Teacher: Your parents had sexual contact as married people. You were born. You were also created in the image of God. Yet, you were born into a sinful world. And since you are a weak human—a finite being—you are going to sin.

Me: I am here accidentally then?

Teacher: No. You are here because it is God's will. God created you just like everyone else.

Me: God created me knowing I would go to hell forever?

Teacher: Not exactly. God offers you a chance to go to heaven by believing in Jesus and obeying his commands.

Me: My options are eternity in heaven or hell?

Teacher: That's right.

Me: Why can't I die and just be dead?

Teacher: Because God created you in his eternal image and loves you too much for you to die like any other animal.

Me: If I died before I was old enough to understand what it is to believe in Jesus, where would I go?

Teacher: To heaven.

Me: Why?

Teacher: Because you had not reached the age of accountability.

Me: I was not very lucky then.

Teacher: Why do you think that?

Me: If I had been miscarried, or stillborn, or aborted, or died of a terrible childhood illness I would have gone to heaven. Now it is a question of whether I believe in Jesus. Beforehand, I would have never known him and still got to heaven.

Teacher: Think about the good things you could do for God in your life. You could be a mighty witness for Jesus.

Me: Can I get by with believing Jesus was a good teacher or a prophet?

Teacher: No. You must believe he was the Son of God and shared the divine nature.

Me: How can I really know this?

Teacher: It's all in the Bible.

Me: So, I have to know what is in the Bible?

Teacher: Exactly and interpret it correctly.

Me: And I must interpret what is in the Bible the way you interpret it?

Teacher: Yes, if you want to go to heaven.

Me: I thought my salvation was based on God's grace?

Teacher: Yes, it says so in the Bible.

Me: What do I do to get grace?

Teacher: Nothing. It is a gift from God.

Me: That is not what you said. You said being saved and going to heaven is based on knowing a specific teaching about Jesus and knowing the real meaning of the Bible. You told me my salvation is based on my *knowledge.*

I cannot say for certain how the hypothetical teacher would react to my conclusion. The one aspect I know about it is the teacher would probably ask the pastor what to say next. My response, as pastor, could be that the standard evangelical teaching about salvation is deeply flawed because it is based on the teachings of St. Augustine of Hippo, St. Anselm of Canterbury, Martin Luther of Wittenberg, and John Calvin of Geneva. The Protestants view salvation as a matter of contractual obligation on the parts of God and individual humans. Anslem of Canterbury taught Jesus' death appeased divine wrath because the divine honor had been offended much like that of the Lord of the Manor or a King. St. Augustine was obsessed with himself.

The Wesley brothers, John and Charles, were perplexed by these same problems. John decided to have faith that God would help him understand it better and do what is right. He knew the facts of salvation. He believed in forgiveness. And he hoped to practice a primitive form of Christianity. Charles wrote hymns still used by many Protestant and evangelical churches. He even criticized his brother. For them theology was not speculative but a matter of practice. An individual person chose God and God's ways. The only person who could choose to save or condemn would be God. It is not an intellectually satisfying approach. It gets the job done, though. For a couple of English preachers, they could not have been more American.

The question of my own faith and belief was raised after all by the district superintendent. I am very familiar with the Bible and the history of how the Bible has been interpreted. I can detect when someone is fudging interpretation to fit a prejudice on their part. I suspect this is why the twelve steps do not specify anything about God or affiliate with any sect or denomination. The question remains, "If God is how I understand him, how do I get an understanding?"

One approach is to have the person visualize or list the attributes they would like to have in a best friend. Once that has been done the person can begin thinking and acting as if their understanding of God is real. This God has every appearance of being an imaginary friend. What if this imaginary friend fails to deliver? Does it become a mere idol? Possibly. Remember though that this imaginary friend is how a person may envision God. Suppose there is a glimpse of the shadow of the real God in that person's understanding of God? If the person has a false understanding of God without any glimmer of reality to it, then the imaginary friend helps to the degree that the person stays sober and follows Dr. Bob Smith's prescription. Under the heading of "Always remember it," Dr. Bob wrote three instructions.

1. Trust God

2. Clean House

3. Help Others

The twelve steps are in these instructions.

When I reentered the SLF/IOP program later that week, I met with Stan who told me the treatment team decided I should remain as I was instead of starting over. I was getting credit for having turned myself in. Most people in my position were usually caught by the random urinalysis testing. My tests were done randomly every Tuesday. We sometimes called it "the whiz quiz." We were watched carefully to make certain we did not cheat the test in some way. I drank on a Tuesday evening. I may have gotten the alcohol out of my system by the following Tuesday. It did not matter. I knew I was not getting any better. My life as I knew it was destroyed. I was not certain there could be any other life.

I picked up where I left off. It was not easy to describe to the others in SLF when they asked, "What happened?" I kept it brief, "my marriage ended, and I drank." I could be more open with anyone that knew me during my stay in the inpatient treatment. I would have to warm up to the others, and most of them were young guys the age of my sons.

A few days into the SLF, one of the other old guys said, "You seem to be very patient with the younger ones."

"I have sons their age," I replied. This was an interesting point that was not lost on me. There were younger guys with me. And I was old enough to be their father. It made my situation difficult. How should I respond to them?

The staff said it was a good thing that some of us older men were among the younger ones. I remarked once how difficult it was to deal with the younger ones when most of them didn't possess any life skills. They often did not know about cleaning and cooking. Yet, we were responsible for our own meals. "We want you older ones to help teach the young guys." I was told. My response was to say, "I am not here to raise anybody." I was there supposedly to get better.

The whole extended IOP with residence on campus was multilayered when it came to patients. The railroad workers or family members of railroad workers who were there for ninety days stayed in the main building where inpatient treatment was. Their meals were provided. The contract with the railroad companies required that. As far as their housing was concerned, they simply continued as though they were inpatient residents.

The next group were the professionals. As I said earlier, these were people who possessed some type of state-issued license for their work. This was a crowd of physicians, pharmacists, lawyers, nurses and one nurse practitioner, and even one chiropractor while I was there. They had their own separate housing. And they were given different IOP classes that were even coeducational. Once a week there was a Professionals Only outing and a special meal provided. Many of my fellow patients asked me why I was not staying with the Professionals group. I said it was because the state legislature does not require any credentialing for me to do my job. The fact that no government board or agency was involved in my profession was news to the people with whom I lived.

The men's housing was an office complex that looked like a strip mall. The office buildings were converted into bedrooms with bathrooms and common rooms. There was only one functioning kitchen between us and the Professionals. We had to work around each other at mealtimes.

Every morning and evening the two groups met for morning spiritual and at evening for "ten at ten." The latter meeting was based on the tenth step "(We) Continued to take personal inventory and when we were wrong promptly admitted it." A staff member would sit with us while we shared around the room how life went that day and if there were unresolved issues that day for any of us. In the mornings we gathered for a rather bleary-eyed devotional reading and then discussed a few plans we might have or goals we wanted to achieve that day. We would leave right after that for morning workout times and then our three hours of IOP. In the afternoons, we went to our service work.

Service work is a big deal for recovery groups. They likely would not exist without it. When it comes to meetings of AA, NA. and other recovery groups, service work takes the form of making coffee, setting up before and cleaning up after meetings, and carrying out the trash. If your home group meets in a clubhouse, activities that help maintain the building are important too.

The service work we were taking on at Cornerstone was where we had been contracted as labor for some non-profit organizations. These organizations take the form of thrift stores sponsored by religious bodies or cleaning a homeless shelter. The druggy buggy would transport us to any of these. We were volunteer laborers who were required to take part. Service work was considered part of treatment. It is difficult to see how it was. The people in charge at the site were not social workers or therapists. They were managers and nothing else.

The cost for housing alone was $800 per month. In that facility, I lived with a bunch of people. I had an uncomfortable twin bed in a room I shared with a railroad worker who decided to stay in treatment until he retired. He claimed it was the only thing keeping him sober. There was a third twin bed that did not have an occupant while I was there. Out of the $800 we each were allowed $30 per week for food, toilet paper, and other necessities. We were encouraged to pool this money that was always in the control of a counselor. There was a weekly shopping day for those who wanted to buy groceries. For some of us, that was all the food we received. We were allowed to go with a group on the weekends to buy anything we wanted that was not banned. I should note here that the single-bedroom apartment

I rented not far from there was $390 per month. Even considering utilities involved, the $800 appeared to be more than the cost of housing us.

One evening a call was made to us that the next day some VIP's would be touring the facility. The staff wanted us to clean the place up. We did so. We organized who would do what and then worked on the building to get it clean. The next afternoon, Tina, one of the senior administrators approached me, "You guys did an awesome job, thanks."

"I hope you get the grant to help update our building," I said.

"No," she said. "We need that money to treat more people."

I honestly do not understand what was meant by treatment. I was performing service work one day at a local thrift store. I was clearing out the storeroom and trying to get merchandise on the floor. These donated items were given prices that were almost as high as if bought brand new. This place was owned by a group that called itself a ministry. I was having difficulty walking. My right knee was hurting. It was very painful. I was used to having pain in that knee because of an accident I had at a foodbank where I fell dropping a dolly loaded with canned beans.

I did what I could that day at the thrift store. The next day I asked for another assignment because of the pain. I was given something called van shadowing. I remained on that duty for the rest of my time there, but my knee pain got worse. The pain was bad when I tried to walk. One of the other patients who had needed to use a cane for a short time gave it to me. I hated trying to use it to walk a short distance. I never wanted to take it with me to any session I attended. The fitness instructor tried helping me to work out in ways that did not require me to use that leg. The knee swelled to almost double in size.

I decided I would talk to Stan about the pain. I knew that Cornerstone offered pain management therapy. It was described as non-addictive treatment. I did not know what form it would take.

"How does a person apply for pain management?" I asked.

"You say, 'Stan, I need to sign up for pain management,'" he replied.

I said it and included, "that was easy."

I thought it would be an added class to the sessions I was already attending. I was wrong again. Pain management was held during the sessions I would have otherwise been attending. The problem was that it was in the building down the hill from where I was. And with a swollen knee, it was going to be as difficult to walk down the hill as it would be to walk up it. The staff had access to golf carts they used to move materials and supplies around campus without needing to use one of the vans. I could hitch a ride on one of those if a staff member went or if someone took pity on me.

Pain management was therapy based on the alternative medicine Reiki. I decided pain management was like the "art therapy" the Cornerstone brochure advertised. It did not really exist.

Earlier, I mentioned that a New Age healer once said I was, as she said it, blocked. The pain management specialist was this healer. She told me her credentials that were, in fact, meaningless and gave me some information about her spiritual journey, which was interesting. I have run into spiritualists, wiccans, reflexologists, psychics, and other non-traditionalists in my time. I have learned to listen rather than argue. I take this same approach with charismatics in churches. Often these are people who fear being ordinary and seek power to separate themselves from the main herd. In this woman's story, there were examples of how connected she was to the energies of the spirit world. Pain management was an adventure into the bizarre. Oddly enough, my health insurance paid Cornerstone to do this therapy. When I asked to see a doctor or nurse practitioner, I was charged my co-pay. Small wonder people in chronic pain turn to these practitioners.

When I went to my therapy session, the healer had me lie on a table while she attempted to use her excess "energies" to move the pain out of my body. She was not a true charlatan. She honestly believed she was helping. She did not relieve my knee pain. She helped my neck pain by using acupressure. And she looked concerned when she got to my knee.

"There's a lot of heat coming off here," she said. I realized that meant infection was involved. "You may want to see a doctor about it." Like I said, she was deluded. Yet, she was an honest person in her delusion. She had the patients' best possible care as her goal.

She said I was blocked when I voiced skepticism during a later class about how quickly the pain returned the next day.

I made a few calls to the medical staff at Cornerstone and my general practitioner's office. Later, I was given an appointment to see a rheumatologist who drained fluid off my knee and shot antibiotics into it. He did not give me any medication for pain. I was glad for that because Cornerstone was strict about pain medication. While I was in IOP, I was able to take my prescribed medicine without a nurse's supervision. My medication was still scrutinized. It was to be expected.

The day I went to the rheumatologist I missed the morning sessions. I was sitting alone in the SLF building waiting for the van to take me to my appointment when I noticed a young guy approaching the back door. Being a former office building the door was steel and glass with large windows beside it that constituted the wall for that side. I was sitting near that wall waiting for the van to take me to the doctor. He saw me and left quickly.

The door locked automatically when it closed. We often kept it propped open so we could get in and out easily. Smokers had to smoke outside the building. The young guy who came up to the building apparently knew that door would be open. There was a crew of stone masons working on the front of the building. I was not immediately suspicious because there were restrooms in the downstairs area. I did not try to let him in because my knee hurt too much. There were other places nearby anyway.

When I returned from receiving the medical treatment I needed, I began my shift of van shadowing. Dave, one of the senior counselors, walked by and noticed the bandage around my leg. "Are you all right?" He asked.

"Yes," I said. I told him about seeing the rheumatologist. I was still bothered by the young guy trying to get into the SLF building. "And there's something else I need to tell you," I said.

It is common knowledge that Rehab centers are good places to get your drug of choice. A dealer would easily learn where to go. During the time I was in Rehab, I knew of three incidences when a patient or a group of patients were dismissed. This was going to be one of those times. The administrators thanked me profusely for speaking up.

I hated saying anything. I was in a situation of us versus them, and we do not tell on us. Several of the younger men in IOP/SLF were expelled. Stan came down with a van driver and a list of names. One guy on the list was at work that day.

Stan said, "Let him know I need to see him when he gets back."

The young guy was someone I got along with and really liked. I had his respect. I did not have to wait long. He got out of his car—a beater if there ever was one.

"Stan wants to see you," I said.

"Oh shit," he began, "I am getting kicked out." His eyes began getting red. He went inside and ran up the stairs.

I went back inside to look for coffee.

My friend came back down after learning who had been taken away in the van. When he came downstairs, he walked over to me. He had regained his composure. He put out his hand saying, "I am really glad I got to get to know you." We shook hands. He left.

I do not know if he learned it was me that alerted the staff (them) about the person trying to get inside. I tried rationalizing my actions. I did not know for certain that the guy was dealing. He could have been there to steal for all I knew. I saw my job as being someone who helped other people. I was not supposed to be getting them in trouble. This was my strategic thinking at work. The fact is that my mind was clearing up. I knew what had to be done even though I did not want to do it.

Knowing people in rehab can get their drug of choice is one thing. Knowing that people die while in rehab because they satisfy their cravings is another. I had seen enough death during my ministry to know there is nothing more tragic than a person dying of despair. It does not matter their age or stage in life. It never makes sense to anyone else. A person takes his or her life either deliberately or accidentally by overdose for reasons that seem perfectly legitimate to them. I could not have done anything else that had a chance of saving someone else's life.

The issue of faith was still working in my mind as I continued to do the work assigned to me. We were given a new book for IOP. *Reinventing Your Life* is an interesting read. The authors described certain life traps called *schemas*. My highest scores in the self-evaluation given in the book were abandonment, mistrust and abuse, dependence, emotional deprivation, social exclusion, defectiveness, subjugation, and unrelenting standards. I was indeed a wreck. I had a lot of work ahead of me. Being on van shadowing for my service work provided me lots of time to read and study these issues. The sixth step reads, "(We) were entirely ready to have God remove all these defects of character." The seventh step then claims, "(We) humbly asked Him to remove our shortcomings." Unfortunately, there is no promise that God does any of that. It was important for us to learn what these defects of character were and where they came from. We had caused a great deal of harm to people because of how we acted out these life traps.

I was not wholly surprised by this list. Studying these topics allowed me to develop my own definition. Schemas are coping mechanisms that eventually become toxic to my life and the lives of everyone around me. As I noted above, schemas are like the "character defects" or "shortcomings" alluded to in the twelve steps. My desire to avoid trouble when a potential dealer came to the door was rooted in my fear of social exclusion. I enjoyed the respect I received. I was afraid of losing it. I was falling into the life trap once again where I feared being the outsider. It hurt too much to do the right thing. Still, it had to be done no matter the cost. That latter thought fit right into my desire to live by unrelenting standards. It was hard to accept that even when I did something morally or ethically right that I was doing something to myself that furthered the sickness of my life. It just about makes one scream out with St. Paul for deliverance from the "body of death." I learned that I needed to continue doing what was right while acting according to motives that had nothing to do with how I sought to promote or protect myself. Life was going to be hard for a while.

The process of unlearning is much more difficult than the process of learning. An addict can unlearn toxic behavior so long as that person does not drink or use. It may take a long time for that person. The Big Book says, "we claim spiritual progress not spiritual perfection."[1] Impatience is one toxic behavior that is shared by all addicts and must be unlearned.

Impatience brings back the discussion about God. Faith is about trust and action. I know there is a lot of recent discussion surrounding faith. Some see it as merely religion. Others see it as allegiance. The point to be made here concerning faith is the personal understanding of trust and patience. If a person declares, "I love you," you either believe it or you doubt it. The reason for doubt is you do not know whether you can trust the person. With God, you doubt whether the person is even there. I do not care how much one may protest, the addict doubts. It is a doubt motivated by either fear or disgust.

Addicts tend to carry resentment about faith or religious belief. "I get more here than I do among those religious people," one may say. "The church people do nothing but judge," from another person can be heard. When the God talk in meetings start many simply tune it out. Religious resentment is powerful. It deals with questions of ultimate existence, purpose, and expectations for life. It is only due to social pressure or fear that a person can really be angry at God and not voice it for appearances sake.

I recall many times when people were disappointed, heartbroken, and angry with how something turned out. One grandmother, talking about the death of her grandchild, said, "It didn't turn out right." Then, remembering she was talking to the pastor, said, "Well, how we didn't think was right." I replied, "No. You were right the first time." I cannot believe anything could be right about the death of a child. I have never thought it was my job to apologize for God. It was not my job to defend God when bad things happened. I was not qualified.

1. *Alcoholics Anonymous*, 60.

Being a clergy person who is also an alcoholic led me into deliberate rages at God. Long journal entries were made where I ranted and raved over being cast off away from all hope and despairing of ever having believed in any God let alone one that hears prayers. It was a crisis where I had to evaluate everything I believed up to that point and lacked the capacity to do so.

The more my head cleared the more I was able to think about my religious resentment. It bothered me to see how the image of the Divine I was working with was simply not the image of God most of my neighbors saw. The view so many people have is a God that is brutal, spiteful, and cruel. The figure of Jesus came into mind for most of them as one who saved them from sin and allowed them to go on being and doing what they would be without ever believing. I think the film *Calvary*, which is about a priest that is marked for murder, demonstrates that people can be awful. It asks the question from the point of the view of many clergy, "if the people in my parish are like this with God what would they be like without God?"

Why does God not fix things? It is because God does not break them. God allows and expects humans to clean up the mess we make. The hard part is accepting that God can only fix people if they want to be repaired. Jesus becomes again the figure where God meets people in atonement. Jesus' death is not about punishment. It is about getting our attention. The centurion at the crucifixion realizes in Jesus' death that he is not what people assumed him to be. And in doing this God declares that our image of the Divine as capricious, vengeful, and ever ready to destroy is only our assumption as well. It is false and harmful. People are hurt by it, not saved.

One evening in the SLF when we gathered for the nightly inventory of ten at ten, one of the doctors saw the book I had been reading. "Reverend," he said, "Are you reading Kierkegaard?"

"Yes," I replied.

"I remember reading him in college," he said.

The book is a collection of spiritual writings by the philosopher called, simply enough, *Spiritual Writings*. It was one of the books allowed while in treatment. I am used to the arrogance of some physicians who believe they know all that is important for life. I am quite capable of responding with the same arrogance. I was curious though what he read from Kierkegaard. He could not remember. He was impressed that I was reading the book. The inherent classism of the division of professionals from everyone else was not only apparent to him, but he also assumed it was his due.

My guess is that the book he read in college was one of the books that Kierkegaard published under a pseudonym. Soren Kierkegaard loved to argue for positions he did not hold as true. Many readers have found ways to poke holes in the arguments and dismiss him completely. Other readers have considered how contradictory an argument from one book was with another. What is often missed is that Kierkegaard published ideas and arguments he held to be true under his own name. I was reading one of those.

I began working then upon a spirituality with a somewhat different base than what I had previously done. I was following a path to relate to the Ultimate Other of the universe that carefully read what the Gospels claim Jesus said.

Chapter 6

The Epiphany

Rehab facilities may not be the best solution for addiction. Rehabs can be safe places if done properly; however, they are poorly regulated. Insurance companies do not review what is being done inside them. There are some abuses and bad policies like the ones I have already described, then there are others that are downright hellish.

An exposé published in 2017 about one facility in Oklahoma called CAAIR (Christian Alcoholics and Addicts in Recovery) showed that no oversight on such places can lead to great evil. This place was called "a slave camp" by a former inmate. CAAIR was started by the chicken company Simmons Foods, Inc. to have a supply of unpaid laborers. Other companies such as bottling plants and nursing homes, benefited from similar arrangements in other states.[1] One patient at Cornerstone told me of a place he went to that required daily drug testing and charged the patients for each one. Such places steal cash from the patients and their insurance companies.

Health insurance companies are often skeptical of rehab centers. Recidivism is a problem. Coverage stops after a certain amount of money has been spent. Many times, a patient is unable to complete treatment. Then rehab centers simply do what hospitals do—they put the patient out on the street. One young man was only able to stay two weeks while in inpatient treatment. It was sad because he really wanted the treatment being offered. Cornerstone would not exist in its present condition without the contract

---

1. Harris and Soshana, "They Thought They Were Going."

with the railroads and the approval of the state to treat the professionals. The twenty-eight-day program exists as it does because of the income. It also means there is no incentive to change or update the treatment program. People are often sent to rehab by either being court or employer ordered, like I was. Others come when they know they have a problem. The issue then is whether the treatment is helpful with so many unqualified people doing therapy and counseling. It makes no sense to have the system of treatment the way it is. Alcoholics Anonymous and Narcotics Anonymous make no recommendation for a person to enter rehab. Individual people within these groups may. The organizations do not, and this distinction is very telling.

Alcoholics Anonymous tells members, "Don't drink and go to meetings," some people include "read the literature" in this advice. Attending ninety meetings in ninety days is also advised, and many courts mandate ninety days to those who are charged with driving while intoxicated.

My time in SLF wore me out. My roommate often stayed up on the telephone at night and slept through the day. He had few classes to attend beyond peer discussions or meetings for patients from the railroads. I did not eat well. I dropped thirty pounds and was tired all the time. Every other weekend I was granted permission to return home. I would arrive on Friday nights and go back Sunday afternoons. "Home" was the parsonage.

A departing pastor usually moves in June. Our system of itineracy in The United Methodist Church often has all pastors move on the same day. Ideally, no church was without a pastor for more than four hours during the change of pastors. I was able to return to the parsonage those weekends to pack our belongings. I was often too tired to do it. I learned later that my lethargy was due to a combination of depression and anemia as well as the problems described already.

My sons and their mother would come in on those Saturdays to help. Often, they arrived in the afternoon when I was exhausted. They would leave if I took a nap. During that month there was not a lot of packing done while I was gone. I don't know why. Because the retired minister replacing me was not going to be moving into the parsonage, I was able to come on a weekend in July to pack. We did not have to have everything out until the end of the month.

I was released from SLF and drove back to the parsonage by way of the liquor store. I drank that night and some the next day. My sons and their mother discovered it when they arrived to help pack. Their anger was understandable. Then something happened that caught us all by surprise.

The congregation's lay leader arrived to inform me that I was only allowed to be there to pack. I was not allowed to spend my nights there. It was the first time I heard of it. I looked questioningly at my soon to be ex-wife. She did not say anything. I took that to mean she did not know.

The lay leader saw that I had been drinking. He called someone to say that he had told me. I began packing my stuff to find a motel somewhere. I was effectively homeless.

"I don't think he should be driving now." I heard him say, "He has been drinking." I continued to pack my bag for a motel. "No, he really should not be driving." I heard him say again.

He finished his call and said to me, "All right you can stay tonight. But I want your key." I took the key off the ring and handed it to him.

"Is there anything I can help you with?" he asked.

I was drunk and angry. I would have been angry without being drunk. I was embarrassed to be without a place to go. "I would prefer it if you left," I replied.

He nodded, "I understand."

It was a bad situation. Here was a person who had been nothing but kind and understanding even when he delivered a message that was hard for me to hear. Asking him to stay with me would have been the smarter approach. I was angry. All my schemas returned and worked together. After he left, I drank more, then everyone left.

I called my father and explained the situation. I could come to his house the next day. I decided to drink until I passed out. My bag was packed already. It didn't work out that way.

The lay leader let himself into the parsonage a few hours later. "I know you are not yourself," he said. "The district superintendent is outside, can she come in to talk to you?"

I agreed. When she came in, I offered her a glass of sweet tea. She accepted. We sat and talked for a while. She was gentle.

I told her I believed Jim had ruined everything. That I should never have been locked up in Cornerstone. I was going to my father's tomorrow. I was sick and near to passing out again. She said that she had another pastor who was also an addiction counselor and asked if he could join us. I said, "yes." They had decided I needed to be taken somewhere to dry out. I opted for Cornerstone because of the infection I had contracted in the hospital while detoxing.

I asked the lay leader to call my mother and father to tell them where I was going. The other pastor helped me into his car and loaded my bags for me. He gave me a small pillow and drove me back to Cornerstone detox. He tried to enroll me for another twenty-eight days and added his own name to those who were to look in on me from time to time. This gave him access to my records there. I only stayed three days.

Stan came to visit me . . . again. He asked me what happened. I tried to tell him but with the new drugs and my condition at the time I could hardly stay awake. It was a good thing the staff woke us in the mornings and came to our rooms for mealtimes.

The medication I was given was different than what I received in the hospital. It was hard to keep going. I did eat at every meal. The nursing staff were good to me. It felt like I was becoming a fixture. One said, "I would rather see you here than dead."

Then, on my third day just after eating lunch, a tidal wave of nausea hit me. I went into the bathroom and vomited. I still felt bad. There was a pain deep in my chest. I asked another detox patient to go with me to the nursing station. I told them what was wrong. They checked my vitals. My blood pressure was too high, and I was sent by ambulance to the hospital. My parents came and sat with me in the ER and then in the room where I slept until the staff took me for tests. I asked my mother to call my ex-wife. Neither she nor the boys would come to see me. If I was going to have surgery, I said, I wanted to see the boys before I had it.

She was too busy.

The tests the following day all came back negative. I asked my mother if I could stay at her house. I reasoned that after finishing detoxing I should not go to my father's place. Both he and my stepmother drank. I was not going back to Parrottsville. I went back to Cornerstone to get my luggage and checked myself out. The medicine had worked out of my system, so I was no longer groggy. I did not want to take it any longer.

My ex-wife called both my parents the day I was taken back to detox from Parrottsville. She complained about not having any help packing. My father who had offered to take the dogs refused to talk to her anymore when she took them to the animal shelter instead. My mother did not want to talk to her either. She had my stuff put in storage and brought a few items to my mother's. She gave me the storage bill. She also brought my truck to me. I stayed at my mother's place for two months.

The August term for my doctoral research was in Atlanta. I stayed in a hotel on campus. We gathered to conduct further research on our projects. We were nearing the end of the program with only one more year left. That year was going to be comprised of preaching class and writing our projects. The students in my academic program knew that of all my difficulties the main one was alcoholism. I had begun to write messages on social media about what was going on with me.

One student who is one of the most compassionate people I have ever known and who has many gifts for ministry, approached me early in the week. He walked over to where I was working and sat down. "How's it going?" he asked.

"I am all right," I replied.

"What are you doing now?"

"I am staying at my mother's right now. I have a medical leave stipend from the church."

He nodded and said, "The UMC does not get everything right. But when it does it does it very well." He grew up in the denomination. Circumstances within The United Methodist Church made it hard for him to be ordained. He went to the United Church of Christ instead and maintains a good relationship with his home congregation in Georgia.

I told him what I had been trying to do. I attended an AfterCare program at Cornerstone and attended other recovery meetings daily. He told me how addiction touched his family. He also told me he keeps copies of the AA big book and the *Narcotics Anonymous* basic text in his office at the church he serves.

I was surprised.

"What's fifteen bucks compared to someone's life?" he asked rhetorically.

It was a good attitude. I, on the other hand, was faking that attitude. I just did not have it. The third tradition says, "The only requirement for membership is a desire to stop drinking." I have been told it used to read, "an **honest** desire to stop drinking," which was later dropped. I can understand it. My desire was to stop getting drunk. I still wanted to drink. I was doing the right things, but the desire though to pick up again was there. I was torn up by everything around me. The week I spent in Atlanta was good for me. School and work were what I needed. I intended to write the perfect paper. I was dry rather than sober.

The story goes that a fellow had not been to a 12-step meeting in a long time. His wife gets tired of his constant snappishness and bad attitude. In exasperation she says, "Either start drinking or go to a meeting. Just get out of this mood of yours." The desire to drink is where the bad mood arises. A dry drunk is more miserable than one who is drinking. While both are miserable people to be around, a dry drunk is worse because he or she resents not being able to drink. Going to a meeting helps one deal with that resentment. For me, it was that I had been forced to do something I did not want to do—being sent to rehab. And, in doing it, I lost what for me was a pastime.

The English have a saying about the parish minister. He is around when we are "hatched, matched, and dispatched." One year, when I moved to a new charge, a wave of deaths took place. I held thirteen funerals in thirteen weeks. In fact, there were two in one day.

Funerals really demonstrate how congregations view the work of the pastors. One friend said, "They want chaplains not pastors." One other colleague said, "They want us on the shelf until they need to take us off of it." Funerals were the best example of that kind of need.

Usually, the funeral service is held on the third day after the death. For a pastor, the funeral begins the moment a person dies or when the pastor is notified of the death. The work includes meeting the family to discuss what they want in the service, choosing the appropriate texts from the Scriptures, making sure everything is coordinated logistically with the funeral home people, and writing and delivering the message/eulogy. I had so much practice that I got quite good at doing funerals. One funeral home usher told me he liked the funerals I did. He said, "I always stay for yours because I learn about the person." That is my goal for every funeral. I want the person remembered. My rule of thumb for a funeral service is "Praise God, comfort the family, and honor the person who has died." Afterward, the families of the deceased usually expressed gratitude and surprise that I really did know their loved one.

The work of a pastor goes largely unseen. I once sat on the Committee for Superintendency in a district. The superintendent presented us with a report of his activities on the job. I got an idea from his example. I would compile that report for myself too. It was not only for the benefit of the Pastor-Parish Committee. It helped me see how my time was being spent. It also helped me understand how much time I was spending on the job.

It was not a flattering reflection. I was putting in the time, sometimes sixty hours a week. I was also neglecting something else.

I was spiritually dry. I could not understand why.

Every morning I read devotional material and prayed. When the weather was pleasant, I would sit on the front porch of the parsonage with Bible and prayer book. I opened them and read them. And I got nothing from them. It bothered me that it was happening. I wondered if the readings were somehow deficient for me. Should I be doing these devotions with someone else rather than alone? Am I faithfully doing my work as a Christian, a pastor, a father, and a husband?

The latter question was the one that could have led me to conclude that my drinking was the big problem, but that path to realization would have required sobriety. I thought the times of the day I did not drink were times when I was sober. I suppose by legal definition it was accurate. Unfortunately, it just was not true.

Ken, our Insurance Coordinator for the Annual Conference, tried explaining it to me. He told me before I entered inpatient treatment at Cornerstone that when I left, I was only starting. "You won't be sober when you leave," he said. "It takes a long time to become sober."

"I have heard about dry drunks," I said.

"That's what you will be. You will need to join a group and work the steps."

My strategic thinking allowed me the time to drink. I was not drunk when I read my devotions. I would have passed a roadside sobriety test. My head, though, was still clouded.

Even if I did not acknowledge it, my brain wanted the next glass of booze. No matter how many hours I was putting in "on the job," I was only focused on the next drink.

Did some of those long hours working on sermons and lessons allow me to take a few sips (or gulps) of brandy? Of course, they did. Should I have discounted them and the sermons I preached from my hours worked? Maybe so. Another drunk pastor trying to recover was speaking at a meeting and told of how he gave such "good sermons" while he was actively drinking. I asked, "Who wrote them?" It got a good laugh and a less than serious death threat from the speaker. People attending recovery meetings laugh a lot. We laugh because what we say is ridiculously true.

People at church would tell me my sermons were good. I do not discount the possibility that I could have said something that was helpful to someone. Listeners attend church seeking to hear something that they want or need even if it confirms what they already thought. And then there is the spiritual aspect where not everything relies on me doing and saying the right things. I knew despite the results a "C effort" was what people were getting from me. I may have worked the hours while only getting by with as little as I could.

I was continuing to have health issues. My doctor told me I was anemic. I was in a lot of arthritic pain. When I asked about living at my mother's house, she promised she would not be around that much. She was there a lot. Her gentleman friend suspended their relationship. It turned out to be a habit. I was quickly becoming her project. She did not have good judgement about it.

Mom held strong resentments against an alcoholic uncle. She thought he was weak. Indeed, that was how her family and neighbors would have looked upon any alcoholic. They assumed such people could do something better. Yes, they could with the right help. And help only comes from someone that understands the nature of what it is to be addicted. She could not look at me, though, as she did her uncle. I was surprised and grateful for that. I push-mowed her lawn and did some other chores to earn my keep. I spent time on the computer doing my schoolwork. I paid my bills with my medical leave stipend. I went to meetings. But I got drunk twice while staying there.

The first time I got plastered while living at my mother's was after a conversation with my ex-wife. She told me that I had been abusive when I drank. She was not interested in trying to patch up the marriage. I called my sponsor and told him what was said. He said, "Just don't drink over it." I already had the bottle. I went to bed before Mom got home. She discovered the discarded bottle in the garbage can a few days later.

The next time was when I decided I did not care if I ever did anything again. I was deeply depressed. I was also angry at everything. I finished the entire bottle, that time. My mother found me passed out on the couch in the living room.

She woke me up. She did not realize I had passed out drunk. She thought the liquid in my glass was sweet tea. She asked if it was all right to pour it out. I groggily told her it was brandy. I staggered to the bathroom and urinated on myself before I got to the toilet. I vaguely remember her helping me undress and get my pajamas on for bed.

The next morning, I woke up hungover and could not eat. Mom always wanted to get me up for breakfast. She told me she had not slept well. She worried about what to do with me. She was both angry and concerned. To top it off, that Sunday was her birthday.

"Should I get a loan so you can go back to Cornerstone?" she asked.

"No," I replied. "I don't believe they would readmit me. Probably just let me stay at SLF. I would be sitting there doing nothing except going to meetings."

"What can I do?" she asked in a voice I considered whiny.

"Nothing," I replied.

I showered and dressed. I was able to drink some coffee and take my medicine. She said, "Let's just make today a starting over." I agreed and hugged her. We went out to lunch with her sisters for her birthday.

I stayed dry in September and worked on my degree. I attended meetings. I talked to my sponsor. I read the recovery literature. I attended weekly AfterCare. I made plans to move out as soon as I could.

I moved on October 1st into a small one-bedroom apartment. I decided low rent and cheap upkeep was what I wanted. I could work in a relatively quiet place. My apartment had the added attraction of being near where I had meetings if I was going to go to them. I started drinking again a week or so later.

I got by for a while with drinking. I did the same thing I did before the intervention.

1. Drink only when you know you will not be driving.

2. Take one or two drinks when the shaking begins.

3. Feel free to drink while reading, writing, watching television, or cooking.

4. Avoid everybody while drinking.

I managed to do a lot of things while still feeling the lingering effects. But I drove after having a drink to stop the shaking. I did laundry. I attended meetings. I even went to the gym. One Wednesday afternoon, hours after a morning drink, I drove to Parrottsville to be an observer and take permission and interview forms for parents and guardians of the children at the after-school program for my doctorate.

I often stood outside before Wonderful Wednesday to meet the buses when the children were let out. This time I remained inside. The children were excited to see me.

"Pastor Don," one of the girls began, "You're back. Are you staying?"

I replied, "I am here to see what it is like to visit." I could tell she was confused by that. "I will visit again in a few weeks." I took some preliminary photographs. I sat and talked with some of the children while they ate. I participated in the circle time for Bible story and prayer. I noted some minor changes to the program that would be included in the project paper, and I left.

I was feeling guilty for drinking that morning. And I was beginning to feel the effects of needing to reinforce the morning drink. Instead, I drove to AfterCare hoping to receive some wisdom. I wound up leading the meeting. I went home and drank. I woke up in the living room at two in the morning. I carried on that way for a few weeks.

I was back on the cycle of needing to drink at different times of the day just after Halloween. I would sleep and wake up to vomit. I was unsteady on my feet most of the time. I did make time to do certain chores. But I was rapidly approaching what I was told would be "right back where you started from."

It is a myth that a person must "hit rock bottom" before they can start getting better. The stories people recovering from addiction tell often imply that myth is accurate. It is not so. It is what a person realizes when they supposedly come to the lowest point in their lives, a place where they cannot go any lower, that matters. I have heard folks say they had not hit rock bottom yet when they went back out into the world of active addiction.

The only true rock bottom is when someone buries your corpse. When you allow your addiction to take your life beyond all hope of recovery and resuscitation, then and only then are you at the lowest you can be.

There have been many people whose lives became more messed up than mine by drinking or using. We often call it the YETs. I have not been slapped with a driving while intoxicated (DWI) charge, yet. Another person has not lost the house, yet. I am not dead by drinking and using, yet. The word is also an acronym for "you're eligible, too." Rock bottom is just a myth. It is a bad assumption on the part of some well-meaning researchers into addiction treatment. When will you have the best opportunity to help an addict recover? When they hit rock bottom.

I finished the last bottle of booze on November 18, 2018. It was a Sunday afternoon. The tremors began that night. I tried to sleep. I was sick. And I kept my phone nearby to call if the withdrawals got too bad. I got through the night. The next morning, I could barely hold a cup and could not eat. Graham Chapman of Monty Python once said when he quit drinking cold turkey at home he experienced "three days of unpleasantness." My mother just happened to call that morning. I asked her to take me to the Emergency Room.

I approached the ER registration desk and explained my situation.

"What do you expect us to do?" one of the two people behind the desk asked.

"I was wondering if I could be admitted to detox."

"We don't do that," I was told.

They took me back to have my vitals checked. I was taken to a room where they gave me an IV for dehydration and then a drug to help the tremors. They observed me for a few hours. A nurse practitioner came in and gave me a lecture.

Mom stayed with me through all of it. She took me to her house as she had been instructed to watch me. If I had any more problems, I was to be brought back immediately. It made sense to do this. Her house was closer to the hospital. Before going though, we went to my apartment and got an overnight bag packed. I made it through the day and night. I was given medicine for nausea. I only used it once.

The next evening, I attended a meeting of the Religion and Socialism Working Group for our Knoxville Area chapter of the Democratic Socialists of America. I was the person who wanted to organize this group for our chapter. Several others, including a retired professor of religious studies from the University of Tennessee, joined in the organizing effort. I felt honor-bound to be there. I had another reason, too.

One member of the group knew my situation very well. And I knew I could talk to him. We spoke off to the side.

"I have been drinking again."

"You have my number, don't you? You know you can call me, right?" he asked. Then he sighed, "How are you feeling now?"

"Depressed and still a little sick."

He nodded. "Next time, call me. Do you have a sponsor?"

"Yes."

"Call him first."

We went back to the meeting. It was an informative discussion about the ministers who came to the area to work among the impoverished people in rural Appalachia. We discussed the history of the Highlander Center. For two hours, my mind was off myself and my desire to drink.

The next day, Wednesday, I went back to my meeting. I told the truth. And while there in the meeting, I found grace. At the end of the meeting, I took another chip to begin the program again. I committed myself to another ninety meetings in ninety days. I went home each day and struggled. I was not exactly white knuckling. I was trying to get through Thanksgiving and Christmas without letting holiday depression drag me back to the liquor store.

Each day for the next three weeks, I would play the tape to the end in my mind. I could drink myself into a stupor and forget everything going on. I would also be in the hospital or jail for doing something while blacked out. Blacking out is a phenomenon where the person is so intoxicated the brain stops recording and storing memories of the event. I used to joke about this state in college. "If you can't remember what you did on spring break, you must have had a good time." It is the same issue when a drunk says the next day, "I don't remember how I got home." It is a dangerous situation to be in. It is baffling, too.

I made phone calls. I was on social media. I was apologizing everywhere I looked. Mostly, I was thinking, mulling things over, and even praying to whomever was listening. I had lost everything. I felt alone and isolated even during meetings and Thanksgiving dinner with my family. Miserable does not begin to describe it. I was beginning to feel the loss.

I had lost my wife. I had lost contact with my sons. I lost my job, essentially. All I had left was my life. Did I want to lose that as well?

This was when I realized where my clouded judgment was taking me. Did I want to die? Hell yes, I did. Why not? I was stuck and running in place. I did not want to run anymore. I was feeling helpless beyond help.

My friend who visited me in the hospital explained, "I was sent to a Navy rehab unit. I knew I had a choice to make. Did I want to stay in the Navy?" He and another sailor decided they did and acted very much like they had been taken back to boot camp. He was saving his job and his future.

I wondered if I wanted to get back into ministry. Did I want to go back to church work? I was working on my first draft of my project. I enjoyed many aspects of full-time ministry. Still, I did not think that would be enough to stay sober. Was I like my former SLF roommate who stayed there unable to do anything else? I did not think so. I could write and study after all.

Did I want my family back? Yes, I did. However, my ex-wife made it clear there would be no reconciliation and our divorce was going forward. My sons wanted to avoid me. I was able to meet with them to give them some money as a Christmas gift.

There was only one thing I had left for me. Did I want to live or die? I knew early in Advent the answer to that question. I wanted to live and to stay sober so I could live. To do that, I would have to work at doing everything I could to become sober.

I started meeting with my sponsor. And I booked an appointment with the conference clergy counselor. I needed three kinds of help to stay sober. First, I needed to work on the steps. I looked at the steps as nothing magical or miraculous. I treated them like a treadmill—it only works if I use it.

Second, I needed the support and involvement of the church. I was not getting any help from the hierarchy. When I saw my bishop, she was good to stop and ask how I was doing. When my district superintendent called, I had to explain to her why I left Cornerstone after the last time. I told her the person who said was a recovery counselor had no credentials. That self-described counselor had tattled on me when I removed him from the list of people to whom Cornerstone could release information. I told her she had set the conference up for a lawsuit that I would never file. It was the fellowship of my local United Methodist clergy that helped. It was not only those involved in recovery ministries.

I went one Sunday morning to Maryville First United Methodist Church. Both the senior pastor and the associate pastor were good friends. A retired UM pastor now passed on to glory, Judith Anna, stood up and called out my name. "Come sit with us," she said. I was glad to do so. Other clergy friends have kept up with me, offered words of encouragement, and advised me. The daughter-in-law of one of my clergy brothers sent me some delicious peanut brittle for Christmas. She told me via social media that my posts inspired her.

Third, I needed mental health care. My general practitioner increased my dosage of antidepressants. I had sessions with the clergy counselor that the conference provides for the clergy members and our families. She has addiction recovery training and years of working in the field. I started seeing her on my seventeenth day of recovery. She assured me that I would be able to get through the difficulties.

My family was there, too. My parents, my aunts and uncles, and my cousins all let me know their doors were open when I needed them. Staying alive was possible, and I was lucky to be invited to so many celebrations during Christmas and New Year's Eve.

I settled on Green Meadow United Methodist Church as the congregation with which I would be involved. Clergy members are considered members of the Annual Conference. We are attached to charges or churches in some capacity either as pastor or as retired clergy. I was appointed to medical leave which made me available. I could be called for any emergency pastoral care if the appointed pastor was out of town. Usually, a retired minister volunteered for that. Other clergy members usually have other jobs that keep them from filling in if need be. I could be available in emergencies and to fill the pulpit if needed.

Christmas Eve that year saw a sanctuary full of people. When the service ended with candles and singing "Silent Night," the usual custom of gathering around the altar in a circle turned into standing along the walls so everyone could take part. It was beautiful.

My father continued to tell me that I was not only invited but *wanted* at his house on Christmas. The same was true of my uncle and aunt for their Christmas Eve day breakfast. The only issue was that both gatherings would include alcohol. I decided to take part and developed an escape plan.

Christmas day at noon a nearby AA group hosted a dinner for anyone who wanted to be there. I brought tea and sodas. We filled the place with people, including some patients from Stepping Stones which was a new Cornerstone program for people who lack insurance. Holidays are often hard for recovering addicts. Sometimes our families have written us off. We need to be family for each other.

I brought ginger ale and non-alcoholic sparkling apple cider to my dad's place. I drank them. I also had a plan for if I was triggered to drink. I parked in a place where I could get out easily. I knew where there would be a meeting going on every hour. Having the plan made me feel secure enough that I would not drink.

I arrived a little early at my father's house. He asked me to come outside. I went out with him. He lit a cigarette and said, "The boys came by earlier to get their presents. Their mother stayed in the car. We asked them to stay so you could see them. They didn't want to. They opened their presents and left."

I was angry. I was hurt. And I believed they intended to make me feel those emotions. I went for a drive up Pellissippi Parkway until I calmed down. It was the route I would take if I needed a meeting. I thought about going to one. I decided their actions were the culmination of complaints they heard about me at home. I did not get over it very easily. My oldest son and I got into an argument on Facebook about it a few days later. Looking back, I believe the only point where I was correct in the discussion was when I told him he and his brother had put their grandfather in the middle. They were not thinking about it that way. Their problem was with me, as they saw it. They are also apples that have not fallen from the tree. I see signs of depression in them. I know how difficult it is to do those things when you are trying most of all to protect yourself.

When I returned, we had the family meal, the presents, and the time together. I was not good company. I enjoyed the pets. I chuckled at the interactions of my youngest siblings. I went home and slept. I was glad it was all over. It was not a Hallmark Christmas. It was an all too real and raw one. The first holidays following the breakdown of a marriage are always the worst, I am told. I hope I never go through it again.

I made no plans to do anything on New Year's Eve. I stuck to the plan.

Chapter 7

Disappointments

LIFE CAN BE VERY disappointing. Inconsistency in other people can be hard to deal with where your own life is concerned. My sponsor said it was my seething anger that was at the root of my troubles. He says he believes this afflicts most members of the clergy and is the reason so many of us do unhealthy things to ourselves. I am inclined to agree.

Clergy people, like many professional people, live lives of disappointment. Lawyers, medical doctors, and public-school teachers suffer from moral injury because the careers they intended to devote their lives to become devastating to their lives. Clergy members are the same. A friend of mine found that being clergy after being a successful engineer did not work out very well. Medical doctors are at the mercy of insurance companies. They pay huge amounts of money for malpractice insurance and then hope the health insurance companies pay up. If the insurance company refuses to pay for a treatment, the doctor (not the company) must inform the patient. Lawyers, despite all our jokes about them, are the protectors of the rights of the people. They only make the large amounts of cash representing the people that wish to destroy the rights of others. If they do not do so, they work eighty-hour weeks to help clients whose rights are being violated by someone. As one friend of mine said, "I will never do it again not in a million years." The public-school teacher too often works for a low salary provided by municipalities in states where some politicians only want to destroy the institutions that improve the quality of life of their communities.

Protestant clergy people live under the assumption that lay people are just as capable of learning how to live in the love of God from their study of Scripture. It is a fantasy. The average pastor is constantly dealing with committees made up of lay people who know next to nothing about theology, the Bible, the history of church doctrine, or even the way the structure of the denomination works. Popular or civil religion usually reigns supreme in the minds of many church members. These are not illiterate or ignorant people. Often the lay members are successful people in business, the professions, farming, or retired from these positions. Many of these people *could* read Scripture, practice meditation and prayer, or learn about spiritual discipline. They convince themselves there is no time to do this. Their lives are full. Middle class people do not live religious lives. The pastor and the church exist for their convenience. The tragedy is that there are so many good people who could achieve great benefits for themselves and others.

An equally tragic consequence is the void left is often filled with people of ill will. For them, the church exists to be their pet project and basis for power. What they seek in a pastor is someone who will take orders. There are some clergy who are so demoralized that they bury their conscience and please such people. Evil often takes over such places and causes harm to many people. One of the saddest occurrences in my ministry was when a family invited me to attend their parents' fiftieth wedding anniversary. The church had been so difficult because the members allowed a small group of evil people to run things. It had been terrible for me. The daughter who invited me said, "Mom really wants you to come if you can. But she also understands if you don't want to." I was disappointed they assumed I was unforgiving. Reconciliation is not practiced by many people who believe themselves reconciled to God.

My sponsor and I worked hard on the steps and on my issues. The day came when he told me at the end of the meeting. "Something has happened to you. I don't see the anger in you anymore."

"What do you mean?" I asked.

"I mean you aren't carrying that cloud."

I understood then. Clouds change our moods and behaviors sometimes. Robert Bolt wrote a scene into *The Mission* where Robert DeNiro's character Mendoza, carries his armor and weapons through the jungle as he travels with the Jesuits to the mission above the falls. The armor and weapons are the tools of his life as a mercenary and slave trader that symbolize his murderous pride that made him the killer of his younger brother played by Aiden Quinn. His penance, which is his choice, is to drag all of that behind him wherever he goes. He is always bound to it, and he chooses to stay that way. My cloud was similar. It was my pain, bleeding, and anger. I was bound to the "body of death."

I was not carrying it that day. Hal guided me in doing the fourth and fifth step. He had told me that I would lose some of the crap I was carrying if I did the steps well. So, I went home and wrote and wrote many pages. The following week I read off the pages. What happened? How was I injured? What was my part?

"That was more thorough than most people do on their first fourth step." He said when I finished. "How do you feel?"

I did not feel any better. "Satisfied," was all I said.

Two weeks later we began discussing the sixth and seventh steps, "(We) were entirely ready to have God remove all these defects of character" and "(We) humbly asked Him to remove our shortcomings." During IOP, I identified at least some defects of character and toxic coping mechanisms. The next step was to ask for their removal.

They were not removed. There is no promise that they will be. I supposed it was a process. I did recognize them. I could identify them when I retreated to them. It was helpful to be mindful about such things. It helped me overcome them more easily. Knowing that helped remove that cloud Hal identified.

We moved on to the eighth and ninth steps, "(We) made a list of all persons we had harmed and became willing to make amends to them all," and "(We) made direct amends to such people wherever possible, except when to do so would injure them or others." I admitted this was probably going to be the hardest step for me to take. I had stupidly ignored advice from many people not to make apologies until I understood what I was apologizing for and could make sensible amends. It brought out one of my character defects.

"I am always right," I claimed.

"How's that been working out for you?"

It was almost a congenital defect. My parents often said that about themselves. My mother prides herself on possessing knowledge. If a person wanted to torture her, all he would have to do is keep a secret from her and let her know he was doing it. She is not shy about sharing what she thinks she knows. My father possesses quite a bit of knowledge about how actions should be taken, how a process should occur, and why it is important. It is useful. And it can be very annoying. I grew up being ridiculed for being wrong about a problem. Other times if I knew how a device or method worked, my parents often dismissed me.

Ridicule and belittling were methods designed to keep me in line with what my parents wanted. I devoted a lot of time trying to be informed and holding onto correct answers. It never served to make life better. I was eighteen when my parents split up. I was exploring most everything a young man my age would. I was going to school without any idea about what I wanted to do with my life. At the time, I was ready to explore. I explored ideas, practices, booze, music, sex, and trying to fit into the world or make the world fit me.

I lived with my mother and my sister. Mom was going through an extremely weird period in her life. She demanded my attention to be on only those activities she wanted me doing. She got back into church in pursuit of a man who had a job that made more money than my father had. The job my sister and I had was to make her look as good to him as was possible. We had to get involved with his family. We had to be at church. I did not go, and it was a major problem for her. Mom was convinced she was going to land this guy.

There was only one problem. The guy had an eighteen-year-old woman in Honduras he intended to marry. He had convinced her family when she was fourteen to raise her to be his wife. He was divorced. He wanted to marry a virgin. He wanted children from a child bride. He did not want a woman who was older than him and had grown children. It was insane.

The other issue was that the church where we were raised hired a retired Air Force noncommissioned officer to be the associate minister. He was a con man. He passed himself off to be a psychologist, a Christian counselor with no credentials or degree. He endeared himself to my mother by saying if his wife died, he would be "beating down her door." It was sick.

Mom became one of those middle-aged women I described earlier that was using church to find a guy. I wish there were a name for that. I think a good term for it is "narcissistic searcher." A person looking for someone who will be a good servant. In the meantime, I was in college and my sister was in high school. My job was to take care of her unless Mom wanted something else from me.

I built up most of my resentments against my entire family during this period. Dad was always showing up at the bookstore where I worked when Mom was angry at me. He was called to talk to me. He seemed happy to do her bidding. He did not like anything I was doing either. I was aggravated and in constant misery. When I did something to help myself that the family did not understand, they made fun of it and me. I had nowhere to turn.

I tried to join the military. Rod, my best friend, had done that and got away. My father went ballistic. He told me about how abusive the military was, that I would be miserable, no one in their right mind . . . and so on. What no one could see was that I was living in an abusive situation. I knew there had to be a better way. I just was not ready to be homeless.

I was always being threatened with being thrown out. The one time I left, Mom went into hysterics. My sister, the majorette, tried to brain me with her baton. I was made to feel guilty. The threat was always made. I knew it would not happen. Mom depended on me to make sure everything worked in her life while telling the family how awful I was to her. I lived through threats of homelessness, threats of suicide, and physical abuse. My father said I was at least getting three square meals (that was not true either).

It was a mess. And it never got better even when I started back to church and entered the school of preaching. It was the worst of lies, and I let myself believe that I was doing the right thing. I even publicly defended my mother. I looked for someone to decide to love me. At the same time, I was suspicious of anyone who said they did.

I lived in that mess for five years before I married and moved to North Carolina to get away from it. I did not know that I could have moved to Siberia and still not have gotten away from it. I was taking the broken person of whom I was everywhere I went. My toxic coping skills, fears, and character flaws went with me everywhere for the next twenty-seven years.

Working the ninth step helped me overcome most of my own brokenness. It seems to be counterintuitive. I wanted people to make amends to me. That is the nature of resentment. Apologies come from people who see they have done wrong. When one is always right and binds their self-worth to that concept, any lie will do to keep them from seeing the wrong that has been done to another person. I needed to make amends for any part I took in situations that happened to me. I also took to heart the clause of the ninth step that reads, "except when to do so would injure them or others." I decided that some situations would injure me further. Other people decided my offering amends would cause them more injury. Most people were willing to give me the benefit of the doubt.

I went to my brother-in-law's auto dealership. I had not spoken to him or my sister for six years. The issue was something I did that for which I felt I was justified in doing at the time. I understood now that I should have kept my mouth shut about the issue. I walked into the door of the dealership.

"Are you lost?" he asked.

"No," I said. "It could look like it though." I chuckled misreading what he was saying.

"It's not funny. You need to leave."

I could have tried to say more. I did not. I left. I was upset. I drove around awhile to calm down.

Dad had encouraged me to reconcile with them. I called him and told him what happened. He was upset by it. He did not seem angry with either one of us. I was already practicing enforcing boundaries with my parents. I needed them with my father as much as I did with my mother. They did not and do not get it. My dad wants to make situations better. He taught me that relationships, like everything else, can be repaired. He also believes people can be fixed. That was what he was attempting to do by showing up to talk to me about the issues Mom had with me. It is a bad approach.

I saw my sister a few weeks later. Dad had spoken to her already about why I went to the dealership. He was interfering. He did not understand that though. I asked her if I could talk to her. She replied, "I don't think that is a good idea."

Hal says I tried. Being willing enough to make amends that you attempt it is the point. Working the steps is about helping yourself. It is not about helping other people love you. It is about recovering who you are supposed to be. I need most of all to keep that in mind. He also tells me that some amends take a lifetime.

What about amends to the congregations I served? I do not know when I started thinking about that issue. Other recovering people make amends to former employers. I suppose it was a natural issue to consider. I went to my sponsor.

"That's something I had not thought about." He began. I could see that the wheels were turning in his mind. "Maybe you could pray about that."

A week later I received a call from one of the lay leaders of a former church. He was checking up on me. I thought it was an interesting coincidence.

"Probably a sign you need to send the letters," my sponsor said after I told him about the call.

I made calls to the lay leaders of my three previous churches. "Do you think it will be all right if I send the congregation an amends letter?" I then explained what the ninth step was and what I wanted to do. "You can share the letter with the church council or the congregation," I said, "Whatever you think is best." They all thought it was a good idea. I cannot say for certain if it was that the congregation needed to hear an apology from me. It may have been they recognized that I needed to do it. It could be both reasons applied.

I got down to writing. I mailed three letters. Each letter was different. Each had some particulars that I remember needed to be said. Below is an example.

Dear Brothers and Sisters in Jesus

I never explained the problem. I am an alcoholic. My family knew I had a problem before we came here. I thought I got by with fooling everyone else. My drinking was progressively getting worse when the Superintendents intervened. Even then getting sober proved to be more difficult than the people I cared about the most hoped. I was filled with anger, hurt feelings, physical pain, and other feelings I did not understand. The Holston Conference has helped me in my recovery process. And I am now feeling and doing better physically, emotionally, and spiritually. I see a counselor provided by the Conference for the clergy. I attend Alcoholic Anonymous meetings daily. I am now coming upon six months since my last drink.

Part of my growing in health in these areas is to reach out and make amends to people I have harmed. The only exception to this is in cases where to reach out again may cause harm to them or others. I know I caused harm to the congregation. I did not do everything I should have done as a pastoral leader and as a friend. I did not even do the best I could. I know I hurt feelings. I know I never rectified some situations. I also was lazy in how I went about many tasks given to me. I got to the point where I would rush through my tasks so I could go home and drink. There were times toward the end where I could not function of a morning without a drink. I deeply apologize for doing these things.

I cannot offer an answer as to why I did them. There really is no good reason to give. I do not fully understand it myself. Please understand that I am sorry. I hope you can forgive me.

Your brother,
Don Jones

The response I received was encouraging. Months later during our meeting for the Annual Conference in June, the pastor who was serving one of my former congregations approached me and said, "That letter you wrote is the kind of letter a Christian should write." I was surprised that a colleague took the time to tell me that.

I have always been conscious of the fact that when a pastor left a charge, the pastor should leave giving a final farewell with the promise of prayers. There should never be a time for the former pastor to return and assume pastoral duties that interfere with the work of the presently appointed pastor. I got permission to return to Parrottsville to continue my research.

I witnessed too many times when a family wanted a previous pastor to officiate at weddings or funerals without being invited by the present pastor. Lay members of the churches never appeared to understand this issue. They assumed they should have what they wanted.

I never experienced a previous pastor sending a letter of apology to a congregation. I was not sure how it would be received by the pastor. This colleague was responding as a fellow Christian should. I cannot say how much my previous failures as a pastor affected the expectations the congregations had for his ministry. I can only hope my good activities could outshine my failures to make any of my successors lives easier.

A few lay people responded. I received text messages thanking me for my apology. One person said it had helped her understand why I failed to do something in my ministry. She now knew how harmful my personal demons were. I could not have helped someone else experiencing addiction while I was actively involved in my own. I took the words sent to me as signs that forgiveness could be made eventually. No one sent a negative response to me.

All groups that meet to help each other know about people who never made it. *Alcoholics Anonymous* claims that those who fully follow the twelve-step path and "program" will rarely fail to stay sober. The medallion I received after completing my first year of sobriety uses this same quote, "Rarely have we seen a person fail who had thoroughly followed our path."[1] I have never heard anyone claim to have succeeded. I find this problematic because the book claims, "To show other alcoholics *precisely how we have recovered* is the main purpose of this book" (emphasis in the original). I wonder why many do not claim to have recovered.[2]

1. *Alcoholics Anonymous*, 58.
2. *Alcoholics Anonymous*, xiii.

One person said to me that when he began recovery, he was told to buy a suit. "You will go to a lot of funerals," he was told. I see three reasons for this advice. People are meant to be in recovery for life. The desire to stop drinking means life-time abstinence. Over the years, those who attend meetings build up supportive friendships. The other issue is that those who fail to maintain their sobriety can die because the disorder is a progressive sickness. People can and do drink themselves to death. The most disheartening reason is that people often become alcoholics because they are self-medicating depression or other forms of mental illness. Recovery groups have a mixed reputation in this matter. Some members believe using any substance negates sobriety. A person who uses anti-depressants, for instance, is still medicating and not dealing with their problems, these members claim. It is the same mistake many church leaders have made over the years telling people the only thing they need is "to get right with God." It is wrong . . . deadly wrong. Most recovery groups rightly claim to help in only one area of a person's life—to stop drinking/using and maintain sobriety. They are not mental health programs providing therapy. People with years of continuous sobriety are still not qualified to treat mental illness. Suicide happens when a person does not get proper help. One friend put it succinctly, "Suicide also means you aren't drinking, but we don't want that." It still happens.

Because of the stated mission, recovery programs cannot push for a social and political change that removes the stigma associated with mental illness. The church can. A clergy friend says, "The church was once into doing healthcare. It should again." She has a point. The church should also push for better quality *mental* health care.

The consumerist attitude that infects American Protestant Christianity makes this almost impossible. The attitude is manipulated because most religious people do not take the time that would allow them to develop Christian spirituality so they can recognize the manipulation. Unfortunately, the Christianity I grew up with and live in emphasizes activities and attendance to the point that there is little room for reflection and repentance. Many people are walking away from churches because they are being made to feel guilty for not working enough. Others flock to churches that merely give them a good feeling about themselves or entertain them.

Churches either practice judgmentalism when it comes to addiction (and other issues) or a live-and-let-live approach that does not allow problems to be acknowledged. Neither of these practices are supported by the Hebrew Bible.

I recall a conversation my mother once had with a church secretary who thought it was wrong to give financial assistance to addicts. "Doesn't that just allow them to stay on drugs?" She asked. My mother was inclined to agree. I was about ten years old at the time. I asked, "What does the Bible say?" The Bible says nothing about addiction. It says a lot about how we should treat other people. The fundamentalist culture dismisses that consideration.

My own disappointments derive from this problem. My wife did not want to approach the subject of how to live with an addicted person. My parents had no idea about how either to step forward or stand back. Church leaders, who are always looking for a more popular need to fill never has learned from qualified counselors, psychologists and psychiatrists, and researchers what to do. When people do not know what to do, they often do the wrong thing.

The disappointment I had the most was being put aside. I had been working with Westpath/Lincoln Financial that oversees retirement investments and medical disability payouts. I was notified that my benefits would be discontinued the following June. I notified my then district superintendent.

I was able to reach her on the first try. "I am ready to come off medical leave," I began. She said that was a good thing. Was I doing better?

"Yes. I am seeing the conference counselor. I am going to meetings, and I am staying sober."

"That's good."

"Normally, I would come for my annual consultation by now," I said. "When can we do that?"

The annual consultation is a meeting where the pastor meets with the district superintendent. It is designed to help the superintendent represent the pastors during appointment season. United Methodist clergy are appointed by the bishop to their ministries annually. They may remain in the same place where they served the previous year, but the bishop must appoint them *again* to the ministry site. The annual consultation is where the pastor advises the Superintendent if he or she desires a different appointment (or retirement, or an appointment outside of being pastor to a church). Congregational committees called the Pastor-Parish Relations

Committee (or Staff-Parish Relations Committee) also advise the Superintendent if they wish to have a new pastor.

It is an advisory meeting because there are no guarantees. The bishop can decide differently. This is due to two issues. Ordained elders in The United Methodist Church take a vow of itineracy. It means if the Bishop of the Annual Conference decides to appoint an elder anywhere, the elder must go to that place to serve. There is an appeal process, but all appeals must be made before the bishop fixes the appointments during the meeting of the Annual Conference. The other issue is that United Methodist Elders among all the clergy are the only ones guaranteed an appointment. We have good job security in other words.

"We can do this now over the phone," my superintendent said.

"Oh okay," I began, "I need an appointment in the area where I am close to my support system. I am in AfterCare at Cornerstone. I have a recovery sponsor in the area. And I am near my family."

"Okay," she said. "What else?"

"It may be best if I did not have all the responsibility of a congregation. I think it would be best to be in an associate minister position if possible."

"Those are rare," she replied.

"I know. That's why I added if possible."

"There is a process you have to go through to come off of medical leave," she said.

"Who do I contact?"

"The chair of the Board of Pensions and Health Benefits in the conference."

"Thanks," I said. "I will do that."

The call ended. I never heard from her again.

I called the chair of the board and asked what I needed to do.

"I am not sure what you should do," he said. "I believe you need a letter from the conference counselor, you are seeing her, right?" I told him I was. "And the Board of Ordained Ministry needs to sign off on it."

"Who's the chair of that committee," I asked.

He told me.

I called that person and asked him what I was supposed to do. "You need to contact chair of the Board of Pensions and Health Benefits," he said.

"He told me to call you." I explained.

"Well, you needed to contact him first."

"I did that."

"And you need to get a letter from your counselor."

"Okay, who do I have her send it to?"

"The chair of the Board of Pensions," he said. "If she thinks you are ready to come back then the Board of Ordained Ministry will need to meet. I can tell you those meetings do not happen often. So, the sooner the better."

I called the chair of the board of pensions back and told him what was said. He still was not sure about the procedure.

"How about I ask the conference counselor to write the letter and send a copy to all three of us?" I asked.

"Sounds good," he said.

The counselor did as I asked. She said in her letter she believed I could go back to work, and that I was doing what I needed to do to stay sober. It was a good letter. The Chair of the Board of Pensions received his copy. I did not ask the chair of the Board of Ordained Ministry if he received his.

I waited but did not hear anything from anyone. I went about my business. I also put in employment applications.

The Special General Conference of February 2019 was a disaster. The political wrangling left a bad taste in the mouth for everyone who attended or watched the livestream. Not only did the people who called themselves traditionalists keep the prohibitions in the denominations Book of Discipline, draconian measures were put in place to punish those clergy members who violated those rules. In addition to those measures, oaths were to be sworn by the clergy to uphold these new rules. The rules would go into effect the following January. The denomination was in new territory. Our Western Jurisdiction had a female bishop serving who was married to another woman. We were going to witness some major divisions take place. Another issue involved who would be eligible to bring charges against a clergy member. It no longer needed to be done by a member of a church in one's own annual conference. A mess was made worse.

I attended a special meeting of clergy and interested lay people that was held in the district where I resided. Representatives from our delegation to the Annual Conference described what happened. Holy Communion was observed. I was not sure about a sacrament that is designed to celebrate the unity of the church being observed then. I hate to think of such an observance as a mockery. There it was, though. We were paying lip service to church unity while knowing the lines of division were being drawn.

My depression got worse. I was struggling to sleep at night and stay awake during the day. I took melatonin at night. I could get a few hours of sleep. But the side effect was to make the depression worse when I was awake. I was trying to fall asleep while thoughts of suicide came in unbidden. I plodded along going to meetings and doing what I needed to do in working the steps.

The week the bishop and superintendents met to project appointments was in March. I waited after that to see if I would receive a call. None came. I called my district superintendent.

"I was wanting to ask if I received an appointment." I already knew the answer. My real question was why had I not been called?

"There isn't anything available," she said. "Maybe something part-time but you would not be able to afford rent and no parsonages would be available."

I was confused by that answer.

Ten minutes later the Board of Pensions Chair called. "I just received a call from the local district superintendent (not my own). He told me to tell you that the cabinet decided to leave you on medical leave."[3]

"Why?" I asked.

I was not the first person to have been placed on medical leave for addiction relapse. "They left Ben on leave for two years. They decided you should, too. Keeping you on medical leave means the conference still pays its portion of your health insurance. Have you not heard from your superintendent?"

"I just talked to her before you called. She didn't say anything about this," I said.

"I don't understand that," he replied.

"Tell me about it."

After that call, I got out the file and called Lincoln Financial. My caseworker was still in her office.

"I just learned that I am being left on medical leave," I said.

"Bishops decide to do that with some people. Your stipend still ends in June."

"Why?"

"Receiving it is based on what *we* decide. You did get the letter we sent?"

"Yes."

"You have an option to appeal before June 30th," she said.

---

3. The Cabinet is made up of the conference bishop and the district superintendents.

That call ended. I decided to call our Conference Health Insurance coordinator. I explained everything. "What do I do?" I asked.

"Find a job," he replied.

"If I am on medical leave because I am unable to work, how is it that I can get a job?"

"Be a counselor for Cornerstone." Too many people assume the best place for someone in recovery is to be employed by an addiction recovery center.

"They require two full years of sobriety before they will hire someone. Then again, it is only if they need someone."

"I didn't know that," he said.

I had to ask myself this question after the call. Does everyone now think I am only useful for recovery work?

Ben had gotten a part-time job at a grocery supercenter. He remained married. His spouse provided most of the family support. I heard about all the trouble it took to get him back into pulpit ministry. I was suffering from severe arthritis and depression. I could not see myself doing that.

I wrote about my disappointment on Facebook. I did not give details beyond that I was not receiving an appointment and my stipend would end. I was job hunting. A few friends got in touch with me. I gave them the details including the confusion. Ben told me that no one in the church knew how to deal with addiction. I agreed.

The next week I texted Lana, the superintendent from my intervention, asking how the decision was made. Her reply startled me. "We never discussed it."

My father said, "They are punishing you for having a disease. How can they do that?"

I was told by a conference employee, "You may have a case for a lawsuit. They can't keep you from making a living." That person asked that I never reveal their name.

When I broached the subject with my sponsor, "If you do that, win or lose, you will never be able to work for the conference again."

My recovery friends were sympathetic. I asked if anyone knew who was hiring. All agreed, including my sponsor, that I was being left hanging out to dry.

I attended a meeting to hear about the next step in the division of the denomination. It was attended by many of my colleagues.

"Are you getting an appointment this year?" one of them asked.

"No. It was decided because Ben was left on it two years that I should be."

"What the hell does that have to do with anything?" he asked.

"I don't know," I said.

Chapter 8

The New Path

I WAS ATTEMPTING TO put together a cheap bookcase when the phone rang. I saw the name and answered it.

"Help me!"

"Excuse me? What did you say?"

"Help me?" This time it was more plaintive.

"Where are you?" I asked.

"I am at my mom's house. I need help. I have been drinking all weekend."

"Why aren't you at SLF?"

"They kicked me out." He had been one who, like me, could not stay sober. I surmised that he was at his mother's house because his wife had sent him packing too.

"Where is your mom?"

"San Francisco. She comes back tomorrow. I need help."

"Okay. I am on my way. Send me the address." I loaded the address on Google Maps and went as quickly as I could. My fear was that he was drunk and more. I wondered if he was using me to find his body before his mother came home. No one is rational when they are drunk.

I found him outside sitting in the driveway. He was smoking. Thankfully, it was tobacco. When I got out of the truck, he embraced me in a bear hug. The alcohol fumes were heavy. People who have been on a bender reek of booze as well as other odors because they do not bathe most of the time.

"Are you alright?" I asked.

"I've been drinking."

"I know that. Have you taken anything?"

"No. Just my prescription."

That information was not as comforting as it may seem. What was prescribed to him? What was it for? Did he take only the proper dosage? And did he overdose accidentally because he could not remember taking it.

He laid his cigarette on the bumper of his car and led me inside. The passenger side fender was smashed. We stopped in the kitchen where he showed me empty beer cans. An empty Jack Daniels bottle was on the counter.

"I poured it all out," he said.

"When?" I asked.

"Thirty minutes ago." It was about eleven o'clock.

"I see. Before you dumped it, how much was left in the bottle?"

He pointed to a spot on the side of the bottle. He had drunk about three-quarters of it.

"When did you get it?"

"Last night. I didn't open it till today."

Was he serious? Was he blowing smoke in more than one way? "Let me see your prescription bottle." I looked the drug up on my phone. It was okay. You could even drink with it. I was relieved. We went back outside to retrieve his cigarette.

"When did this happen?" I asked indicating the fender. The lights were in pieces. The fiberglass was showing.

"I don't know," he said. "It happened at West Town."

"You were drunk then, too?"

He nodded, taking a puff.

"I guess the police weren't involved," I said.

He shook his head. I surmised he simply hit something in the parking lot of the mall and took off before any call could be made. I checked the back end of the car to see if his license plate was still on. It was.

When he finished his cigarette, we went back inside to talk. He got kicked out of SLF because he drank. His wife would not let him back in the house. He had called his mother who said he could stay at her place while she was gone.

"Did you call your sponsor this morning?" I asked.

"He fired me," he said.

The whole situation was a mess. He had no idea what his mother would do when she got home. She would not find him dead. That was the only good thing I could see. I knew he had a few hours before the booze wore off and withdrawal would begin.

"Can you stay with me today and tonight until my mom gets home?" he asked.

"I can't," I began. "I haven't been sober for very long myself." I take someone in need very seriously. I also believe compassion literally means to "suffer with" someone in need. The only person who is said to suffer *for* someone is Jesus. The problem many clergy have is differentiating between the two. Experience has taught me the difference.

"Who can?" he asked plaintively.

I changed the subject. "What happens when you are in withdrawal?"

He shrugged.

"Do you shake?" I asked. "Do you break out into sweats? Are you sick to your stomach?"

"No." he said. "I haven't eaten anything today."

I nodded. I looked around the living room and saw his partially un-packed bags. "How about I take you to detox at Cornerstone?"

"I don't want to go back to that hellhole."

"I understand." I replied. "But I can't leave you here. I can't stay with you. I can call an ambulance for you."

"No!" he said.

"I can get you something to eat on the way."

"Okay," he said. He packed up the rest of his bag.

He chose the nearest fast-food place. While we were eating, he asked, "You aren't going to let go of this are you?" He meant taking him back to Cornerstone. I believed he needed to go.

We arrived at the check-in point. Stan, the counselor, saw me. He came up and asked what was going on. I indicated my friend. "He is in bad shape. He's been on a weekend bender."

They took him back to finish checking him in. One of the administrators took me into his office with a senior counselor. "What happened?" He asked.

I told the story. I wondered if they thought I might have been drinking with him.

"You did the right thing," he said. "You did the best thing you could do."

We left his office. The receptionist said my friend was outside smoking. When I went to the men's designated smoking area, he was not there. I looked in some other places he could have been. I went back inside.

"He's not out there, "I said.

She was surprised. She glanced to the corner. "His bag is gone, too." She called to see if he had been taken in yet. He had not been. He had run.

We went outside to see. The receptionist saw him pulling his bag across a parking lot across Alcoa Highway from us. I went inside to find the administrator. I told him where my buddy was. "I'll go get him," I said.

I never found him.

I went back to Cornerstone. I learned that the people at intake had tried to get him to commit to another twenty-eight-day stay. He told them he would go smoke and think about it.

I was bewildered. Why was it so important to get him to commit to something so he could receive medical treatment? I left there mad as hell. He would not answer my phone calls. He never has since.

I finished the bookcase when I got home. I spent the rest of the day fuming over the problem. How could they—the people who saw this sort of issue every day—not recognize an escape? Did they not understand a drunk person is not thinking rationally? It made no sense.

Since it was a Wednesday, that evening I went back for AfterCare. The person that oversaw it said, "How are you doing you twelfth stepper you?"

"What?"

"I said, twelfth stepper."

I got what he was saying then. I had done the twelfth step. "Having had a spiritual awakening as the result of these steps, we tried to carry this message to alcoholics, and to practice these principles in all our affairs." I disagreed. The twelfth step includes ideas that I certainly had neither experienced nor done. I saw my actions as helpful and self-protecting.

The administrator from earlier saw me. "We spent all afternoon looking for him. We couldn't find him. We think he may have called someone to come get him," he said.

I was glad they had looked. Their conclusion seemed logical to me. I still was not happy with it though. I later learned that he had been visiting some meetings. I hope he is well. We offer a hand to everyone looking for help. It is up to the suffering person whether they will take it. St. James warns, "your anger does not produce God's righteousness."[1] Being angry over a situation one cannot do anything about makes no sense in the long run.

I reflected on this issue and talked about it with my sponsor. If my resentful anger was subsiding, then what would replace it? Whatever it was, I knew I was on a new track. I was not "back on track" as some would say. I really was doing life differently than I had any time before getting sober.

I know that sounds like it makes even less sense than being drunk. My son had said while I was drinking, "You are not the same person you were before." I understood that. But the fact is that I was the same person while drinking that I was before picking up the first drink. It was where I was going all along. And I now know there was nothing going to stop it without proper mental and emotional health care.

The examples I had in my life were either take absolute control, always have the right answer, or fix the situation to make peace. None of those actions ever really worked for me even when they had the appearance of doing so. I have an example of what I mean.

One Thursday morning, I arrived at the food bank to a hero's welcome. Thursday was the busiest day at the food bank. We began loading boxes of free food into people's cars at 10 am and finished when we were done. Forty to sixty orders would go out. Each client was given food once a month. That morning, I was the hero of the week.

I was also on the board of directors because I was a pastor at one of the churches that sponsored the food bank. One wishes that feeding hungry people was simply something one does. It would be easy if all we had to do was hand out food and then go home, but there must be a way of handing out the food that is consistent. Resources must be managed. And there must be coordination with receiving food from the donors as well as using donated funds to purchase food from Second Harvest and the U.S. Department of Agriculture. There must also be a method or methods of reaching out to people who need food in the community. Organization and administration are important parts of the operation. My preference was to deal with the people being served and the ones doing the serving. I often missed monthly meetings of the board because of my drinking.

One other reason I missed those monthly meetings (aside from the fact that it interfered with my drinking) was that there was a member of the board, a retired businessman, who would go around on Thursdays while we were loading up boxes with food and pull other board members aside one

---

1. Jas 1:20.

by one to pitch his proposals. It was an effective tactic. It was also annoying to be interrupted from the task at hand. I would skip the board meeting because it basically was being held already.

A new issue began to really cause problems for the operations of the food bank. I decided to go to the meeting because I was specifically asked to join it. I was irritated and resentful when I arrived.

American retail marketing uses the motto "the customer is always right." That sentence is ingrained in our thinking as a truism to maintain and increase sales. Customer complaints are injurious to a seller. It is also practiced whenever someone is asking someone else for money to do some work that does not involve selling. What is the donor getting or sees being done with his money? Ministries are not retail or charitable businesses and should never work that way. When ministries are approached in such a manner, punishment and incentive are replaced with guilt. This approach was the cause of the problem many board members and other volunteers were experiencing. Declaring "We aren't doing enough" or "We could be better or more" is an avenue of guilt motivating the volunteers. Those volunteers who recognize the manipulation become disgruntled and stop volunteering. I opened my mouth in protest.

"The point of Christian ministry," I began, "is to build and rebuild community. That means we practice *mutual* ministry based on the New Testament idea of brotherly love. When our practice allows clients to help in serving, they find an extra way to participate in the ministry. We should not try to stop that. Often, these are the people that make *better connections* to the people being served because they are volunteering to help while waiting for their own food boxes. We should not put more burdens on people who are volunteering."

The irritating board member brought his wife to the meeting. It was the first time I had seen her. She was not involved in the ministry. "Which one's are more important?" she asked another guilt-laden question.

"Neither one is more important in mutual ministry," I replied.

Later, one of the other board members lowered his head and voice to speak to me during the meeting. "Thanks. Those were good words, and you are so right, too." The meeting ended with the motion being voted down.

The next day the irritating board member sent his resignation email to all of us citing how mean we were and how shabbily his wife was treated. "Good," I thought, "No dealing with him anymore." Unfortunately, it did not end there.

Two days later, another email went out to us saying since no action had been taken on his resignation, he would rescind it. I was bombed when I read it. I replied with an angry email of my own. I was done with him, I said. I was not his pastor, which meant I, for one, did not have to put up with him anymore. I pointed out that a person who quit because he could not have his way and falsely accused other board members should never be allowed back on the board. I hit SEND. The president of the food bank replied to it the next day saying that the resignation should be accepted.

Many board members congratulated me on standing up. The irritating guy's pastor thanked me for helping him out of a politically thorny situation. I was hugged by the wife of the chairman of the food bank board. Her eighty-year-old husband was ready to quit to end the stress. She was happy that he did not need to do so. I was the hero. I was also drunk when I did it. And that kind of praise goes to one's head faster than alcohol can. I did the right thing, but I should not have done it while inebriated and my judgment impaired. The praise encouraged me to lay down the law and put other people in their place at times when I should not have done anything. It was the encouragement I needed to make a drunk post on social media criticizing my bishop and her husband. It was wrong to say what I said then.

People who are neither addicts nor alcoholics do not understand that the thinking processes of a person in active addiction are not what they should be. They understand that a person should not make decisions, like deciding to drive, while impaired. They do not understand that the person has bad judgment when they are not impaired but regularly get drunk or use. Addicted people who actively abuse substances are rattled by issues concerning money, relationships, and general living. It is hard for to understand that the substances being abused are key to making bad solutions. They cannot see that they are causing the problem. The drunk replies to such challenges narcissistically. Drunks believe they are in the right and know what everyone else should do to make their lives easier.

Am I claiming such people are not responsible? No. They are. I was. But there is no sense of responsibility in the person. They cannot take responsibility for their actions because they are blinded by the need to acquire more of the substance they abuse.

The blackout stage in inebriation is when drunks cannot remember what they did or said the day before because they were so impaired that their brain apparently ceased recording events. Such a person may be guilty of many actions, even serious crimes. They may even serve time in jail or prison for them. They are also incapable of experiencing remorse for an action they cannot recall. They cannot truly take responsibility for the action. It is a pathetic state in which to be. One could sympathize with a person in that situation except for the fact that the person chose to take the first drink. How many times have I drunk to forget the painful situation in which I found myself? Did I care how much worse my desire to "forget" made the situation? I can say I am fortunate enough not to have done worse than I did while drinking.

Abstinence from addictive substances is the only safe way to avoid falling back into a life that brings about these problems. Some alcoholics claim that they have become able to drink socially or responsibly. I hope they have. I accept, for myself though, that I should not try. I was sick. I do not want to be that way again. I will do what I can to avoid it. However, that desire does not keep me from wishing I did not have to be abstinent.

Thinking I could try drinking again or using another addictive substance is why a new way of living must be found for the person who wishes to recover. Twelve step people call this, "living by spiritual principles." Skeptics who are addicts initially balk at the idea of adopting "spiritual principles" or ideas about God, religion, or the supernatural to recover. If such spirituality is important why then, did I become an alcoholic? It is a natural question. All actively addicted people experience dryness or sense of hollowness in themselves. Part of the reason for their drinking is to cover up that feeling.

I prayed every morning. I read the scriptures. I sat outside on the front porch and watched the birds and squirrels. I tried to meditate. I took walks occasionally. I talked with my wife. I was known in the community for being outside every morning doing these things. Internally, there was no sense of grace, sabbath, being forgiven, or even being useful. Drinking was my daily goal. I am certain many of my clergy colleagues can use alcohol and be spiritually filled. I cannot. I see now that I was never fulfilled spiritually before I started drinking.

I have heard many recovering alcoholics claim to have a new spiritual life and to claim they were probably alcoholics before they began drinking. Perhaps this is true. I do not make the latter claim, but I have a new spiritual life. I am not only not the same person I was when I was drinking. I am not even the same person I was *before* I drank. I am surprised by this fact. How did it happen?

A bankruptcy lawyer I know calls her practice "Fresh Start." It is a good metaphor for someone recovering from addiction. Bankruptcy allows an indebted person to breathe a little and start to rebuild their lives. Recovery does the same thing. A person wanting neither to use nor drink again starts over from where they are. Often it is after some great loss—career, good name, family, freedom, or personal injury or guilt. A person begins both where they are and at the beginning.

Spirituality is an important aspect of being human. Human cultures thrive with spiritual centers looking for a sense of transcendence. Personal spirituality is connected to the spirituality of others. Being spiritual means having a way to express one's own spirituality. Spiritual practices or disciplines give rise to expressions of art and rituals. Human cultures all have festivals and fasts. These expressions of one's spiritual culture are important. Jewish concern with instruction and piety mixed with identity as a people brings grace to the world. Islamic artistry based on the written word and the five pillars spiritual practice created a culture that excelled in philosophy, mathematics, trade, and architecture. Christian spirituality has brought about special forms of visual arts, storytelling, and speculation in the sciences. European culture and the cultures brought into the Americas are the fruit of this intermixing of spiritualities. This is only one example of spiritualities at work in cultural expression. I am more familiar with my own background.

Cultures live based on spiritual principles. Personal spirituality is ultimately derived from one's own culture. Atheists are correct when they claim that personal spiritual experiences match a person's culture. If a person in England claims a spiritual experience, that experience has a Christian flavor to it even when it is not experienced by a Christian. The same happens in other areas of the world. Muslims tend to wash their hands before handling a Quran. I have seen Christians in predominately Islamic countries express similar reverence before handling a Bible. Anti-religionists are wrong to advocate the removal of such practices to free human minds. I have noticed the same people use ideas that are inherently Christian to explain morality and life in community.

Being a person who is not a stranger to prayer and meditation, I balked at first. Why did I become a drunk while being someone who prayed and studied spiritual subjects? It was my burning question.

I needed most of all to look very deeply within my own thoughts and ideas about being human. Months before going to rehab I made a simple outline for a project on the definition of what it means to be human. I looked at those notes and references. Friends made other suggestions for reading. My sponsor told me that I was privileged because of the United Methodist Pension and Health Benefits program to be granted a monthly stipend. "All you've got to do in this time is work on yourself," he observed.

There is more to being human than things of the spirit. Alcoholism and addiction take physical tolls on people who actively pursue their drug of choice. Paying attention to my physical health was paramount as well. My doctor's office scheduled an appointment for me. I was required to do this by Cornerstone before I was released. When I went, a battery of blood tests was run. They were not all good.

I was anemic. I was losing red blood cells somehow. A take home test determined the loss was in the digestive tract. I was sent to a gastrointestinal specialist. I was diagnosed with esophagitis as I said before. I had to take powerful antacids to help heal the ulcers in my esophagus. Esophageal cancer is one way many alcoholics die. Most people only associate cirrhosis of the liver with alcoholism. Alcohol works on many of the organs associated with digestion. Diabetes, pancreatitis, gall bladder disease, liver failure are all possibilities. Then there are the diseases associated with cardiovascular health. We often hear of another alcoholic dying of heart failure when we know the return to booze was the cause of the heart problem. Alcoholics have been known to die from hemorrhages because of the weakening of the blood vessels and the constant thinning of the blood.

Being able to work on myself was a good opportunity while I had it. But, when it came time to consider how I would live when the cabinet did not see fit to give me a pastoral appointment, the danger of failure became clear. I had already seen it happen to many of the people with whom I had been in treatment. Some went back to work immediately and quickly fell into old habits because they were unable to deal with the stress and the work environment where co-workers drank or used. It was difficult for them. I wondered about my limits.

Finding a means to live was a high priority in my life. The problem was that I could not let the anxieties involved in doing so rule me. If they did, I was likely to fall back into despair and drinking. I had to make some moral choices. I knew it was not just a matter of possessing the right attitude. I was going to have to make some radical changes in how I went about life. It required moral commitment.

The first commitment is honesty. Addicts and alcoholics are not known for our honesty. We made a life by lying during our active addiction. We lied to ourselves about why we drank or used. We said that we were misunderstood, mistreated, or in need of special help that the drug of choice provided. We claimed that we were just too sick on Monday mornings after a weekend of binge drinking to show up for work (or to pick up the kids, or keep an appointment, etc.). We said to ourselves and others that we could or would cut down or quit drinking. We said there was no problem with our drinking. Everyone else was unhappy because of the choices they had made. If they had only listened to our wisdom, then everything would have worked out, and we could be left alone to our bottles of recreation.

I remembered trying to get this point across to a boy who was in the habit of not doing any task he was asked to do. He would lie about having done his homework or a household chore. His father was not sure how to approach the matter and asked if I would help. I decided the issue was a lack of honesty on the young boy's part. I explained to him about how one lie leads to another and failure to do a task requires a lie to excuse why it was not done (the dog ate my homework) or to cover-up the situation (let me borrow your answers).

Honesty is a moral value. Trustworthiness is a character trait. Investing faith in someone's word is a requirement for social living. Therefore, honesty is a necessity of life for the individual person as well as the community. An unfortunate truth is that honesty fails to be valued when another person or a group of people are prejudiced in some way. Another truth is how many people are incapable of seeing themselves in a bad light and resent those who point out their missteps and flawed actions. People, as we have seen, do this very easily while they are in active addiction. If they never accept the truth about themselves or their lives, then they will one day drink or use again. Honesty becomes a matter of life and death for that person.

Projection is a symptom of dishonesty. When a person cannot accept or admit what they would see in themselves, they will project that negative truth onto another person. These actions happen in all relationships. A spouse may project their faults onto the other spouse. Or a parent may do this to a child. Coworkers may project jealousy onto other people in the workplace to feel better about themselves. A counselor can even do this to a patient. Projection is insidious. It took me a long time to learn that when I was accused of some wrong attitude or action that I did not commit, the accuser was likely experiencing the guilt themselves and looked for a means to alleviate the feeling.

Projection is an example of a manifestation of dishonesty that is not easily recognized in oneself. My commitment to honesty meant serious reflection on my own feelings of guilt and how I dealt with them. It could be done in various ways. One method is writing down how I am feeling and what was done involving that feeling and exposing any resentments. It also helps one see the real motivation behind one's own action. I have heard many people say, "I have often done the right thing for the wrong reason." Discerning our motivations provides insights that can be uncomfortable, yet it helps us see how irrational some of our actions have been. The second step speaks of how a higher power is needed "to restore us to sanity." Sanity is too technical a term for my purposes. I prefer to say my next commitment is to rationality.

Rationality is a technical term, too. Allow me to do some unpacking here. Being rational is more than what many call being reasonable which implies lowering one's own expectations. Rationality is a necessary character trait for living. Being rational means that one does not give in quickly to prejudice. A truly rational person asks if a statement is true. Honesty is involved in that question. Many people conduct their lives based on asking how something would benefit them. It is a hierarchy of needs question that we have become accustomed to asking. Will I get what I need? Will I get what I want? Will this put me in a better place financially, socially, or in good standing with authority? How might I use what I gain for future advantage?

People in active addiction ask questions that put themselves first. The important difference of needs versus wants and what future benefits are involved become jumbled in the psyche. The soul is in turmoil because of this confusion. This statement does not imply that people who ask these types of questions are addicts. They are likely on the border of something bad for themselves, though.

Asking for truth before all other issues is the means to recovery. Rationality is derived from testing the conclusions we think are true. Alcoholics Anonymous has a practice that allows for this to happen. If a person believes that they possess the self-control to drink responsibly, that person is encouraged to go try it. If they can do this, there is no problem. If they find that they cannot drink or use responsibly (i.e., without getting inebriated), then they should be rational and honest enough to admit there is a problem. Should such a person try it again? What would a person rationally conclude?

Rationality allows people to disagree on what is true. Is there a definition of truth that satisfies everyone? If so, then at least some of those people are not thinking rationally. They may be trying to fit into a group. There is a failure within some recovery groups, religious groups, and political organizations that there must be conformity of thought to maintain group cohesion. Such organizations cannot stand. Human beings honestly cannot agree with everything they are told or taught.

There are some people who are contrarian for its own sake. They are people who thumb their noses at everything. They sabotage other people by demanding attention for themselves. A contrarian who is very good at their own special narcissism will eventually demand other people think as they do. They become an authority on some subject or group of subjects while questioning the rational conclusions of the accepted authority. Conspiracy theories work this way. A charismatic person goes around speaking nonsense to anyone who will listen until the listener seeks the approval of the new teacher. The student of the narcissist has given away rationality and is tricked into believing that they are thinking for themselves. The convert needs reinforcement of their beliefs. And, like an addict, imitates the contrarian who uses lies, deceit, bullying tactics, and other forms of coercion to show at least to themselves that they are true lovers of truth that everyone else is either denying or covering up. The contrarian may be a person who has expertise in some field of knowledge. It is often not the field where they level their criticisms. If a law professor with great legal achievements and insights decides to become an authority on curing cancer, that person is just such a contrarian.

Rationality involves thinking in ways that find what is true and then what actions are true. Often a person will not attempt to test their ideas. Other people may have to demonstrate the conclusion for them. The person who can use the experiences of other people to understand truth is a person who learns.

Learning is a value that should always be held and used. I once witnessed a gentleman stop my grandfather from making a dangerous mistake. I did not know the man who helped us. He was not an authority figure in my life. My grandfather though was an authority figure in my life. My grandfather thought he could make a quick fix by simply nudging a belt back into position on a running engine. He almost tried it. He imagined how that should happen. The person helping us physically stopped him. He understood that the rotating pulleys would turn the stationary screwdriver upwards and possibly harm someone. The lesson my grandfather, an authority in my life, taught me that day was to listen to the words of someone who might know better than you. As the old saying goes "two heads are better than one" unless of course neither of them knows anything about the situation.

Learning and being teachable is important. "The beginning of wisdom is this: Get wisdom, and whatever else you get, get insight."[2] There really is no one who is more stupid than the person who believes they know everything they need to know. I once had a person say to me during a discussion on religious living, "All I need to know is that I am saved." I did not reply. The cue was given that the person was done with the discussion. If the conversation had continued, I would have asked the following series of questions.

1. How do you know you are saved?

2. What is the evidence of your salvation?

3. What evidence do you demonstrate that you are saved?

A friend once put it this way: If you were arrested for being a Christian what would be the evidence against you? The only evidence would be your own confession. The inquisition looked for evidence that otherwise banned Jews and Muslims had not truly converted to Christianity. They looked for any distinctive actions that showed they practiced their former religions. Refusing to eat pork was a good one. Keeping religious observances of the former faith were others.

I notice so many friends my age that only half-jokingly say that they need a twelve-year-old to show them how to operate their electronic devices. The smart phone is smarter than me. Included in the admission is also a certain sneer. We older people are occupied with much more important activities than gaming or fiddling with phones and computers. We say by the joke that electronics and new skills belong to children. When we do that, we claim that learning something new is somehow beneath our dignity. We become fools that refuse the call of wisdom.

Putting it in those terms sounds harsh. It is meant to be. Being unteachable is ridiculous. Many people find themselves becoming unteachable addicts and alcoholics. I recall during a rant when my elder son stopped me and said, "Let me pour the wine out." I allowed him to do that. Then I went into the kitchen to retrieve the stem glass and poured another helping. "The

2. Prov 4:7.

dog returns to its own vomit," and "The sow is washed only to wallow in the mud" are quoted in 2 Peter 2:22. These proverbs are on par with "There's no fool like an old fool."

A person who is honest and rational must value learning and be teachable. Finding my way onto this new path was especially hard because I had been fooling myself for years. I thought I was already on it. Once alcoholism began to take over, I began the actions of deception that were dressed up as protecting the family's privacy. The deception began not just with me. I was enlisting my children and wife into the practice. When I started deceiving people, I told myself it was because my family lived in the fishbowl of a parsonage family. Pastors and their families can live in a community where they know only a handful of people. But everyone in the community knows them.

I recall being introduced by the district superintendent to a new charge. Word got out that there would be a new pastor arriving in the summer. Then the news spread that the PPRC would be meeting me and my family. I noticed when we walked to the parsonage to see it for the first time that a woman who lived across the street from the church was standing at her fence watching us. I waved to her. She waved back. Later, I learned she did not attend that church. We were already being watched. I was used to it, but I did not like it.

Being already addicted to booze, the fishbowl existence was something I came to resent. My children hated moving every three years. My wife could never hold a job to give us a reason to stay in one place. Part of the reason for that issue was that clergy families can suddenly move. Hiring a clergy spouse as a teacher in a public school could be inviting instability for the school year. I did not consider that this was an issue for many professions. My younger son's teachers changed three times in one year.

When I began making amends to my family, I was warned by my sponsor that they may be lifetime amends. I realized after considering the problem of how practicing real integrity would begin that process. It meant I could no longer hide in my usual places. I could not hide at all. Honesty, rationality, and being teachable also meant humility.

Humility is neither humiliation nor something placed on one by circumstances. Abraham Lincoln is often said to have come from humble beginnings. I remember my maternal grandfather when he first heard that President Lincoln was born in a log cabin in Kentucky. He was amazed. I overheard my aunt tell my cousin, "Daddy only got to the third grade in school."

Humble beginnings do not mean a person becomes humble. Often it means just the opposite. A person who grows up poor from a family that has lived in poverty for generations can become the most egotistical person you find. Egoism is a response to humiliation. Consider the following statements. What is implied in them?

1. My daddy crawled up out of the coal mines.

2. We came straight out of Compton (or the trailer park).

3. I earned a doctorate from the southern ivy league when my grandfather only got to the third grade.

4. I am the child of a poor immigrant and now own a chain of restaurants.

These claims describe admirable achievements, and all of them can set one up for a fall. Egoism, pride, and hubris are ultimately destructive. Responding to humiliation with hubris is deadly. It is an attempt to survive the humiliation. When it truly becomes toxic, it turns to hate. We hate the person or the circumstances that have humiliated us. And we turn that on people who instruct, lead, and truly know what to do. The person suffering from such toxic pride accuses these other people of being know-it-alls, smug, and even egomaniacs.

My father and I have a running joke. Dad says, "I am always right." I reply, "Only when you agree with me." A friend recently said, "I have heard you both say that." He began, "I just now have figured out you really are." When you familiarize yourself with the laws, bylaws, instructions, or the manual, you know what is going on and what to do. It is quite simple. It is also rather humbling because you know the solution did not come from yourself.

A recovery platitude says "There is no one too dumb to get this program. But there are a lot of people too smart for it." I did not understand it at first. I saw it as an attack on what I thought was my integrity. Being willing to learn means being humble enough to ask for help. I learned after much trial and error I was not going to walk the new path alone.

Chapter 9

Restoring the Ministry

RECOVERING ADDICTS OFTEN SAY, "It's a good day to be clean." Many people outside the recovery community are familiar with the phrase "clean and sober." What does it mean to be clean in this sense? Simply put, it means not using our drug of choice. Later in one's recovery the meaning changes to include how one is living new attitudes and a new spirituality.

Sobriety is just the same. First, a sober person is one who does not drink each day as they come along. However, if the person does not try to work the steps or otherwise get their life in order, then that person is said to be dry rather than sober. It sounds strange to us. We can ask, "Why can that person not stay sober?" It is a phenomenon of falling back into every old habit without drinking. It can make a person and those around them very miserable. The Narcotics Anonymous book says it plainly, "Self-obsession is the core of our disease."[1] It is this self-obsession that brings about the misery to ourselves and other people.

The priestly code placed people, animals, and objects in three important categories. These were unclean or defiled, clean, and holy. Almost everything and everyone was in each of these categories at different times of the day. A person could be considered clean when they wake up in the morning. The same person could do something that defiled them and later could be restored to a clean state. If a person prepared for a sacrifice or was

1. *Narcotics Anonymous*, 55.

otherwise dedicated to the service of God, that person could be considered holy once the preparations were made.

Daily Christian prayers preserve these categories. A person confesses sin. The same person prepares to pray and hear or read the Holy Scriptures. And then they end with mutual blessings between themselves and the divine. Defiled by sin in the beginning, restored by confession and pardon, and then blessed beginning the day.

The argument is made that these are merely ceremonial categories. Implied in such a statement is that ceremony is somehow impractical. Christians might claim they could, in good conscience, violate the rules regarding clean and unclean foods because, for the Christian, God had "removed the ceremonial law but kept the moral law intact." But a rabbi would ask, "What makes you think it is ceremonial?" Good question. How we eat is just as much a moral question. After all, is the social prohibition against cannibalism merely ceremonial?

The point is that being unclean, clean, or holy are states of being and living that are supposed to have practical effects in the lives of people. Living by spiritual principles and practices is important for the lives of human beings, especially for those who have habits or addictions that could end their lives. Spirituality is essential to existence. It is true that the individual person or the community of persons require a transcendent aspect of life. Participating in activities that enhance one's spirituality is strongly advised for anyone who wishes to recover and overcome.

I thought hard about how I could overcome spiritual dryness. As I said in the previous chapter, I thought myself spiritually healthy. I even thought about those activities related to worship, preaching, teaching, and church administration were evidence that I was taking care of that side of my life. I had witnessed other clergy who became caught in their own struggles with moral and physical failure. Many of them in their attempts to recover from the losses tried to be more than they were beforehand. Sometimes they manifested more conservative evangelical ideas. Other people would go toward theological liberalism. A few others would give up on their faith entirely. I had traveled in all these camps at one time or another. I was sure I never really wanted to be in any of them again. I could not go to these places looking for a cure.

I was, in fact, already where I needed to be. I was studying practical theology for an advanced professional degree. Christian history shows that the church has usually believed based on how the church prayed. The saying,

"The law of prayer is the law of faith," governed how the great theological concepts were developed. Another point to be made here is very Wesleyan. The actions of the church communicate what the church believes. Better known as "practice what you preach," the New Testament book attributed to St. James the brother of the Lord instructs Christians to demonstrate our faith by our works. Having faith takes work. St. Francis is attributed with the saying, "preach the Gospel at all times and when necessary, use words."

I did not change my daily practices. I gave more attention to them. Early on I found that another United Methodist clergy person hosted an online prayer group every morning. I made it a point to try to take part on the days I did not oversleep. People joining the group each day shared their concerns and requested prayers. Many people believe having prayers said for them affects their situations. I understand their view. I was impressed though by the fact that my day went better simply knowing someone *cared* when someone else struggled. I would ask for prayer when I was feeling low, really struggling to stay sober, getting ready to fill the pulpit for a friend, or being in pain from illness. I stopped taking part in that group practice after a few months. It helped me overcome my feelings of isolation. I decided to reach out to friends locally and my recovery group.

The other issue was the church and my role in it. I was not sure what that role would be. I began attending Green Meadow United Methodist Church in Alcoa. I preached a few times to satisfy some course requirements. It began to become more and more like home for me.

One cold February morning I walked briskly from the parking lot to the church building. A couple of greeters were standing inside. "Hi Don," one began, "Where is your coat?" I was being scolded for leaving my coat in the pickup because I did not want to take it inside.

I had not been there for a few weeks. I often visited around. The pastor said, "It's good to see you here."

The person who previously greeted me chimed in, "I told him he always has a place on our pew." Yes, this was the same person who scolded me earlier. I was considered by them, at least, to be home. I decided to stay and get to know everyone better. I had friends who attended there. I had in a sense been evangelized by the congregation as well as my brother and sister clergy members.

I got a message from another friend from the Strength for the Journey Committee that I had once chaired. "Would you be open to serving on the design team for the camp this year?"

I hesitated. "I will do what I can," I was told when the first meeting would be. Being on the design team did not necessarily mean I had to attend the camp. I was not sure if I wanted to or if my schedule would permit it.

I decided to make an appointment with the district superintendent in my local area. John agreed to meet with me. We met for lunch.

"What do I have to do to return from medical leave?" I asked.

"Well," he began, "you have to first have a year of sobriety."

I was closing in on five months at the time. "Okay," I said.

He continued. "Then we will need to get the medical proof that you are ready to return."

"Like what? A letter from the conference counselor and my doctor?"

"Yes. And from any other therapist you are seeing. Then, we may only give you a part-time appointment at first to see how you cope. We really do not know for sure. We are trying to develop a policy."

"I see."

"You are helping us do that. We may even ask you to review the policy when we have it written."

"Sure," I said, "Anyway I can help."

John had given me enough to digest for the time being. It was suggested it would be in my best interest to participate in an upcoming required training regarding the church sexual ethics policy. I took this advice and registered for one of the sessions. Our conference does that every four years for reasons of liability for clergy malpractice claims. I was not going to be eligible for a pastoral appointment. I thought having credit helped both the conference and me.

I violated a typical recovery advisory. I met a smart and lovely woman, Kathryn. I began seeing her and we developed a relationship before I had a year of sobriety. My sponsor told me, "Well, I decided months ago you were going to do what you wanted to do." Kathryn knew many of the same people I did. Her best friend from college was a guy I grew up with. We marveled at the idea that we never met when we both attended that college. Our friend even worked with me during that time.

The recovery advice on relationships was during your first year of sobriety to get a houseplant. And later you might get a pet. If they both live, you can begin dating again. My landlord did not permit pets. And I managed to kill the plants I took over after my neighbor died. Kathryn and I did all right, though.

Even with all the good things happening for me, I could not shake the nightly dark thoughts. I had anxiety about what I would do when my stipend ended. The worst part was realizing each night that I had unbidden thoughts of suicide. They took many forms. I thought about the various means I could end my own life. I was shocked to find thoughts of hanging myself show up when I was putting clothes on hangers in my closet. Thankfully, I did not own a gun. I did not think any of my friends or relatives would allow me to borrow one. I was in dangerous territory and did not know what to do about it. My general practitioner changed my medication, but the increased dosages did not help. I lived with these thoughts for months.

I avoided isolating myself by attending recovery meetings every day and sometimes twice in a day. I talked to Kathryn every night. We saw each other when we could. I had a presentation for my degree to produce and deliver in April and graduation in May. I had plenty to do. I was looking for a secular job. I was not sitting alone and brooding. It was depression that had a physical cause. Relief came from an unlikely place.

I filed an appeal to reinstate my stipend. I did not get a hearing/interview until a month after it stopped. The interview was done over the phone. I had been placed on medical leave because of my drinking. I was not doing that. I did not know what would happen.

"Why do you need to continue receiving the stipend?"

I explained my problems with arthritis. And then explained my nightly bouts of the dark thoughts.

"What are you taking?" the committee asked.

I told them.

"Who prescribed that for you?"

I explained my family practitioner had increased my dosage. A psychiatrist contracted to Cornerstone had first prescribed the medicine.

"What were you taking before?"

I told them.

"For how long?"

I told them. No one was asking about my arthritis pain. I found that odd.

The call ended with the nurse saying she would call back in a day with the ruling. She called three hours later. The stipend would be extended. But I had to see a "competent psychiatrist" within the next three months and send proof of it. I think the word competent was used to make sure

I did not start working with a psychiatric nurse practitioner. My health insurance only had nurse practitioners in network. I called a recommended psychiatrist only to learn I would not get an appointment for four months.

I went outside the insurance venue. I decided to pay out of pocket. I chose a psychiatrist who was taking new patients. She changed my medication to a different drug and then experimented with the dosages. I started having the thoughts less often. It was not easy. She eventually got me over the problem of the unbidden thoughts of self-harm or worse. The light was gradually overcoming the darkness. But the out-of-pocket expenses were hard on the budget.

I approached the insurance company about the problem. Was there a way to receive reimbursement? The best the insurance would do is persuade the doctor's office to file a claim with the insurance company. Then, they added the expenses to my deductible. I appealed. I explained how I had been mandated to seek out a psychiatrist. It allowed me to see how much a physician is paid to help someone with mental illness. Honestly, I would not have taken the one-third payment the insurance company offered.

The mental health crisis in America is just what I described in the above paragraphs. It is an impossible struggle to find good practitioners who will work for almost nothing. Health insurance companies do not cover most forms of therapy except for prescription drugs. I am glad they do that. It makes one ask what the standards of treatment are? If the problem can be dealt with by medication, there would be no crisis. There would be no specialization in psychiatry either. The reviewers with Westpath understood the need. The health insurance company did not understand anything except for the policy.

Drug and alcohol addiction treatment centers have the standard twenty-eight-day program for treatment because that is all most insurance plans consider to be adequate time. Researchers in the field note this fact. Why is treatment considered complete at the same time insurance will not continue to pay? Many other patients opt for a ninety-day program if their insurance companies can pay for it. I wondered if I would have benefitted from the ninety-day approach. Now, I don't think I would have. As I stated earlier, I was not convinced enough that I wanted to live. The question remains, "Are the insurance companies right to be suspicious of extended approaches to treatment?" The popular ideas of twenty-eight days or ninety meetings in ninety days have no research supporting them. The claims that they work are based on patients self-reporting. These approaches are not even described as necessary by twelve-step programs.

Mental health is a broad area of medical practice. I find it difficult to say that every claim to the amount of treatment a person needs is legitimate. Rehabilitation centers are good reasons for some concern about effectiveness and the expense of the treatment received. The mere fact that some have been shown to be little more than scams attests to a need for regulation and oversight. And yet, professional medical doctors specializing in this field should be considered competent by the third-party payers.

Psychiatry has those who are skeptical of the effectiveness of the discipline. The Church of Scientology opposes the practice. Many churches hold to some degree of views that mental illness is either a separation from the divine or demonic activity. Then there are the patients themselves. I have engaged many people in pastoral conversations who thought they were receiving help from a professional counselor. They often leave saying, "Thanks, Don. I would rather bring my troubles to you than pay a shrink." On the one hand I could be offended by being used in this way by someone who desires free mental health care. On the other hand, I know now how expensive such treatment is. I inform the parishioner that they have been receiving a pastoral conversation from me. I am glad to help people in this way, I say. But I am not a counselor. You do not receive counseling during this time.

Professionally speaking, unless a clergy person is a licensed therapist or counselor, they should never say they offer counseling or therapy. It is morally wrong as well as legally wrong. I do not dispense medical advice or write prescriptions for medication. I should not think I can do the other either. The magic word "refer" is important at this point. Just as my doctor said, "If someone sitting in your office told you what you are telling me you would say, 'contact your doctor.'"

I feel the same way about twelve-step groups or religious bodies telling people to avoid mental health medications. They have no business continuing to harm people who need such help. One recovery group often tells a misguided alcoholic that we help a person maintain sobriety. The twelve steps are not meant to cure or alleviate depression any more than they are meant to cure cancer. In other words, go to your doctor's appointments and take your medicine.

This interlude on finding proper care brings us to the issue of stigma and the ideas of being holy, clean, or unclean. I will use another example. If a patient is diagnosed with lung cancer and has been a smoker of tobacco, what do we assume about the person? We may claim that since it was this person's choice to smoke that the person deserves to be sick and to die. There is a stigma attached to smokers. It is such a bad stigma that many of the rest of us believe that receiving second-hand smoke is somehow worse than deliberately drawing smoke into one's own lungs. We want to claim that a smoker is so immoral in choosing to smoke tobacco that that person is endangering the health and lives of everyone else in a way that is more dangerous than to themselves. Smokers are stigmatized in this way. It is the exact same way that people with HIV/AIDS were stigmatized in the late 1980s and still today with some states wanting to charge an infected person who has sex with non-infected person with assault or even attempted murder. Disinformation is at the heart of these stigmas. In Biblical terms such a person would be classified as dirty or unclean just as lepers were thought of in the first century A.D.

"A leper came to him begging him, and kneeling he said to him, 'If you choose you can make me clean.' Moved with pity Jesus stretched out his hand and touched him and said to him, 'I do choose. Be made clean!'"[2] The gospels have many versions of this story. Mark's account is (pardon the pun) rather touching. Jesus touches a leper, but Jesus is not rendered unclean. The leper is healed. And he is healed by something that normally would never happen. Only another leper could touch him. Consider another incident in Mark.

"Now there was a woman who had been suffering from hemorrhages for twelve years. She had endured much at the hands of many physicians and had spent all that she had; and she was no better, but rather grew worse. She had heard about Jesus, and came up behind him in the crowd and touched his cloak for she said, 'If I but touch his clothes, I will be made well . . . Jesus turned in the crowd and said, "Who touched my clothes?"[3] Again we see that Jesus is not rendered unclean by the touch of a social outcast considered unclean. Jesus cannot be made any less holy by this physical contact. These examples should tell us something about the practice of stigmatizing other people.

It is believed by some that the legend of St. Francis of Assisi receiving the signs of the wounds of Jesus called the *stigmata* grew from depictions of him in later life with bandages on his hands. The bandages are explained

2. Mark 1:40–41.
3. Mark 5:25–31.

by the legend. But the wounds that were bandaged are more likely resulted from St. Francis' work among lepers. If this explanation is true, it is a curious connection between the word stigma and stigmata. Would a leprous saint have been a scandal? Maybe in that time it would have been.

People in the recovery community are aware of the stigma that the "earth people" or "normies" put on them. It is hard to acquire employment if a job recruiter learns you are a newly recovering addict or alcoholic. Danger is assumed. Churches are especially sensitive to the stigma of addiction. That is why it is easier to take punitive action against an addict that lies during an intervention. Defrocking is easier than restoring, and it is not meant to be a malicious act on the part of church leaders to do this. Among the issues involved, a loss of professional confidence in the pastor is a major one. I certainly could not be sent back to the churches I had harmed by my behavior during active addiction. The concern remained that if I were put into a parish too early, I would relapse and cause the problems again in a new place. I cannot blame a church leader for their perspective. An unhealthy pastor can make an unhealthy situation for the congregation. The only blame to be given is the lack of a guiding policy on what should be done. "I have never had to deal with this situation before," was the claim of my superintendent. I do not doubt it. What was forgotten was, I never had either. It made for a difficult situation that resulted in disastrous mistakes that are hard to forgive.

Having time to get better helped greatly, and my lay and clergy partners in ministry helped too. I was given encouragement to fill-in preach for some. I was asked to join the Design Team for Strength for the Journey. Simply being on the design team helped me think in terms of doing ministry as a part of my spiritual life.

The job of the design team is to work with the camp directors and registrar to develop the programs, recruit staff members, and set a theme for the camp. This is all done in coordination with the board chair. The hardest part for me that year was dealing with the chairperson who got stuck with the job because I dropped it due to my drinking. He wanted me to take part. I did it to make amends and find healing. And then the question came up. "Will you be able to be at camp?"

I was not sure how to answer them. We were working on staffing and filling the roles of assistant group leaders and outdoor activities coordinator. Until my stipend was renewed, I could not answer if I would have the time.

We discussed what roles I could take if I attended. There was one task that I seemed to be perfectly suited for.

"Could you do a twelve-step meeting for camp?"

Having a twelve-step meeting while at Strength for the Journey had been suggested by some of the campers when we read the evaluations from previous years. We had not yet provided a time for such meetings. I do not know why we never did. Many of the campers had been in recovery for years. One woman showed us an article from the Nashville paper about her nine years of sobriety, living with HIV (now undetectable), and being active in both communities. During the one visit I made the previous year, one gentleman—knowing my situation—asked, "Do you remember when I came here two years ago having taken my last drink on the first day?" I replied I did. He reached into his pocket and showed me his two-year AA medallion. Another camper in recovery, with many years of sobriety, asked me if I would be back the next year. I told him it would at least be a week where I wouldn't drink. He nodded and added, "We'll kick your butt for you if you need it."

It appears in hindsight that we should have welcomed and made space in the calendar for one of these people to lead one meeting at least. None of the staff had ever admitted to struggling with addiction before. We did not know how twelve-step meetings worked. They are most of all voluntary programs. Leadership is also voluntary. Like many people outside of the addiction recovery movement, we were ignorant of the importance of the volunteer aspect. We assumed a sense of control was involved. We forgot the cardinal rule that ministry should become mutual.

When I was asked to lead with a recovery minister, I understood that the Design Team was investing their trust in me not to do something that was outside the pale of the goals of the camp. As bizarre as it sounds, I understood that. And then we decided which twelve-step approach to take in meetings. The rest of the team left it up to us. The hands-off approach was wise. We decided to hold the meetings for those campers and staff who wanted to attend during what was otherwise designated as free time.

We waited until the meetings began to ask those who attended if it would be all right to open one of the meetings to other campers and staff who were not in recovery. We thought it would be a good plan to help those "earth people" understand what addiction was and how the program was supposed to help. The board chair opted to attend. We answered his questions as best we could.

"I was with you every week for a year," he said to me, "and I never knew anything was wrong." He was referring to our clergy covenant group. The Annual Conference of our church strongly recommends that clergy members participate in some sort of accountability group. Methodism began as a group of students forming a club to read the Bible and discuss their spiritual practices including helping the poor. The classic question asked of the participants was "how is it with your soul?" The bishops' attempt to recreate this among the clergy assumed that we would answer truthfully. In this way we would be holding each other accountable to the preservation of our ministries. I do not want to disparage this approach. For an addict, there is little accountability in it. We will not be truthful. Our great temptation is to demonstrate that we hold everything together in our lives and manage life remarkably well. The first step breaks that illusion. In short, the others were not ever supposed to know there was a problem. I was content to die while pretending.

"You weren't at fault for not seeing the problem." I replied. No one was at fault for not seeing it. For those who did, they were not at fault for failing to get me to understand it. The issue of accountability or responsibility in the life of another person is hard to comprehend. Some say, "I am wholly responsible to see that the needs of another person are met." Another person says, "It is none of my business." There are variations of what ethical considerations are involved until the dog is tired of chasing its tail. I am responsible if I fail to do what I can do. If I fail, the failure is forgivable. St. James says, "Anyone, then, who knows the right thing to do and fails to do it, commits sin."[4] It is very plain, but it is not a license to indulge in either recrimination or guilt.

I am sure that friends and family felt something was wrong with themselves when they missed the fact that I needed help. I probably would feel that way too. It is difficult when one cares about another person to accept that there was something about the person that was destructive. There is a sense of grief involved like learning a friend has a terminal illness. It does not need to be there.

My role in the camp was more than holding twelve step-meetings. I was made outdoor activities coordinator. These were also free-time activities. So, I juggled the time involved to do both activities. I settled on two games—cornhole and volleyball. No one was interested in volleyball.

---

4. James 4:17.

I could have sold sets of cornhole games, though. One camper who never played before played every day and decided he would get himself a game when he got home. One camper who loved pitchin' horseshoes warmed up to this game nicely. One half-blind woman stunned us all with her accuracy.

Cornhole is an easy game to play. Basically, it is a bean bag toss. The player aims for a hole cut into a board that is raised at an angle. I have been told the name comes from the Amish who played it using corncobs instead of beanbags.

The third role I was given was to help manage a regular group meeting for the campers. There was an issue with a few of the campers that required someone else to get involved. I was asked if I could lead the evening devotionals. I preferred the new task, too. It helped me get back into the practice of developing a short lesson and delivering it. My skills were there. My practice of them was not too rusty, if the post-camp evaluations are to be believed.

Strength for the Journey 2019 went very well. The weather was pleasant. The atmosphere was genial. And the program was good for everyone. Luckily, I did not have to share my room with Mark for long. He was only able to stay a few days. I was able to retire to my room when I was not needed and when I needed to rest. My arthritis pain would come back when I was fatigued. I worked on my lessons during those times and napped.

A good clergy friend to Strength for the Journey is always asked to come and tell stories and lead a worship time. Being near the Great Smoky Mountains National Park gives our camp a uniquely Appalachian flavor. Our campers come from all over the United States. Many return to camp from year to year. He has become a highlight of camp for most of us. He researches, learns, and tells stories of life in the area. This year he concentrated on the tales that originated in France and were brought by settlers to the mountains. The hero of the story is a trickster named Jack. Yes, Jack and the Bean Stalk comes from that tradition. We were treated to some of these tales. He once said to me, "You know, I tell that story you told me about the one-hundred-two-year-old grandmother. People love it." I now tell people that I give him some of his best material.

The story was related to me by a church member who was telling a class about her husband's grandmother. She must have been something else. She lived to be one hundred and four. And she would say things like, "When you get to be my age, you have to eat dessert first because you don't know if you will be around for the rest of the meal." The story I was told was about her one hundred-second birthday celebration. When she was given a piece of her birthday cake, she was asked to make a speech. She looked around at her family. She saw her children, their children, and her great grandchildren. She saw their spouses, and a few nieces and nephews. She then said, "I guess my momma and my daddy, my brothers and sisters, and my friends must all think I went to hell."

As the day was winding down and the storyteller was getting ready to return home, I saw him as he was leaving. I was sitting still in the hallway trying to keep the pain at bay a little longer. He had been serving as a district superintendent when I went on medical leave. He knew something about what I had been through. He also knew I was not required to take part in any ministry. "Hey, Don," he began, "thank you."

"For what?"

"For doing this right here." he replied. I was thanked for doing my ministry. I do not know why I was surprised, but I was.

"You're welcome." I managed to say.

It was the middle of October. I was a month away from my one-year mark in sobriety. When I returned home, I gave the whole issue more thought. A couple of weeks later I called my new district superintendent.

"Hi, Don. What's going on?"

"You remember last Spring you told me I would have to get a year's worth of sobriety before I would come back into the appointment process?"

"Uh yeah."

"Well, in a couple of weeks, on the nineteenth of November, I will have that time in."

"Congratulations."

"Thanks. I got to thinking about how I am supposed to prove it."

"You have a sponsor, right? Been attending meetings, and working the steps?"

"Yes. I have a sponsor and have been working the steps. I attend meetings at least five times a week. Sometimes twice in a day."

"That's great. And you have been going to counseling?"

"Yes. Every month."

"Good. Can your sponsor write a letter?"

"I suppose so. But my sponsor is a member. I would be asking him to break his anonymity."

"Oh, I see," he said. "Don't they give you a coin or something?"

"Yes," I said.

"Bring that with you to my office after you get it on the nineteenth"

"I can do that," I said. I decided not to tell him that all I really had to do to acquire a medallion was buy one. It would only be proof if I was being honest. Then again, if I was being honest, I would not do that. It was really my word that was important now.

Integrity was the means to restoring my ministry. If I was honest with my sponsor, my counselor, and my doctors, everything could work. It sounds simple, but it took me almost two years to comprehend.

When I presented my medallion, the superintendent made a photocopy of the front and back. He instructed me to ask the conference counselor if she would send a letter to him and the Board of Pensions and Health Benefits for the Annual Conference. I looked up in the Book of Discipline what I had to do. No one had said anything to me last year. I decided this time to look up the procedure.

Chapter 10

Looking for Open Doors

STRENGTH FOR THE JOURNEY was an open door for my work. I needed others as well. Once my Doctor of Ministry project was completed, I wondered what I would do with my time. I attended recovery meetings. I wrote a few bad science fiction short stories, and I exercised from time to time. I had little to keep me busy.

There is a difficult waterway to navigate when a clergy person finds themselves on the outs with the church at large. Who are you during those times? Clergy people are dedicated to the work of the church. Even bi-vocational pastors find themselves to be more rewarded by the work to which they are called. The other job is to make a living. There are those who enjoy the labor for their daily bread. In their way of seeing things, they are fulfilling their calling at the same time as they work outside the church setting.

A clergy labor activist tells the story of helping organize a coal mine strike in Virginia. They occupied the mine for a few days until their demands were met. There were ninety-nine miners and him. When the strike ended, a reporter asked him what it was like to be a pastor among the miners.

"Wait a minute," he began and then turned to the group of miners, "How many pastors have we got here?"

Six miners raised their hands. He knew what the reporter did not know. He knew pastors were not necessarily those people who waited to come off the shelf on Sunday mornings. Some of the best works those pastors did was sharing the burdens with which the miners lived. I doubt the other miners were surprised by the six men who raised their hands.

Bi-vocational ministry is not easy. It requires more stamina and patience than a pastor working full-time usually needs. I recall needing to find something to fill up my time when I was full-time on-call in ministry. I tried volunteering once at a local zoo. I was forbidden to do it by my district superintendent. I looked for more ministerial opportunities like working in food banks and serving on local improvement committees. Many of my colleagues joined police or volunteer fire departments as chaplains. I did not take that route because the requirement to turn out when called to a fire or other emergency would be difficult with my ever-increasing drinking. I helped a church member coach baseball when he came to me one Sunday. "I need help," he said. Those words were my cue. I still could not find interesting volunteer work that was appropriate, but there was often no real challenge. Boredom took over.

When I worked for Levi Strauss and Company in the mid-nineties, I was faced with many challenges. The first was the apparent conflict between my ministry to a small country church and my work schedule. My job required me to work some Sundays. I had flextime in my work schedule that allowed me to do serious juggling with my responsibilities. I had only one problem. I worked on Saturday nights. My shift ended at 2:30 on Sunday mornings. Church was later that morning. I was allowed to come in a little earlier on Saturdays because production schedules did not matter very much on those days. Often, I went in early and left early on a ten-hour shift.

I did not write sermons while I was at the plant, but I thought about them a lot. My job skill was recognizing how to use the space on a marker layout. Many times, I would move the outlines of panels, hip pockets, risers, belt loops, and watchpockets into the spaces without thinking about them. So long as the marker spliced, I was good to go.

I wrote sermons and worship bulletins on a Brother electric typewriter/word processor at home. My wife and son went about their day around me. On Sunday mornings, I took them to our home congregation for Sunday school and worship, then I drove to Williamson Chapel. Two hours later, I returned to pick them up. I lived with a tight schedule. My wife was home all day with our son. She tried to allow me time to rest and work before going to the plant in the evenings. It was helpful, but I could not satisfy everyone's wishes.

One woman at church complained that I never spoke to her, and she would not return while I was serving there. She and her husband attended Sunday school at the church. They never remained for worship. I would arrive at Williamson Chapel during the closing few minutes of Sunday school. I would then set up everything to conduct worship. Both she and her husband would leave. Somehow it became my fault for not speaking to them according to their schedule.

The worst time was when I could not help a friend. I worked in a cubicle with its own dedicated telephone line. It was convenient. I shared this number with the people at church as well as some friends and my family. One evening I got a call from a close friend.

"Hey," he began, "my grandmother just died. We are wondering if you could do her funeral."

"I'm sorry to hear that," I replied. "When did it happen?"

"Yesterday."

"I see. When is the funeral?" I was crossing my fingers hoping it was not going to be an evening service.

"Tomorrow night at Miller's Funeral Home, 7 o'clock."

It was twenty-four hours away. We had been working a lot of overtime. The funeral was to be on Friday night. I was really pressed on how to make flextime work. Getting to use it was seniority based. I looked to the board to see who would be off. My heart sank. It was possible, but with one person already off that day, it was going to mean a twenty-four all day for me before Sunday morning. I made my decision.

"I am sorry. I can't do it," I said. Immediately, I added, "I'm really sorry. It's what I hate about being bi-vocational." I was not sure if he understood what I said. He was neither a minister nor a church attender. I wondered if I was the only pastor he knew.

"That's okay." he said. "We have someone else we can call. We wanted to ask you first." It was a load off my mind.

"I am sorry," I repeated. I find myself from time to time wondering if I did the right thing. My father scolded me about letting down a friend. I was able to be there for that family on other occasions when I was in ministry fulltime.

Another time our department entered into contract negotiations. I was asked to serve on the negotiation team for three important reasons. The first was that would represent the night shift. The second was that I was a college graduate working in a department where there were not any others. And third, I already had a reputation for not putting up with a lot of nonsense. My bosses knew my don't-you-dare-lie-to-me demeanor very well.

When the NAFTA[1] related layoffs came, I had the least seniority in the group. I already had my plan made to take a "student pastor" appointment at a three-church circuit in Sevier County. I had the scholarships I needed to get my Master of Divinity. I was on my way to ordination in The United Methodist Church. Then a monkey wrench was thrown into the machine.

The plan was for the layoffs to take place in stages. The first stage was the week of July 4, 1999. Three people would go at that time. I was definitely going. Then one of my coworkers got angry from all the stress and uncertainty. She was volunteering to go. In fact, she was exercising her rights to demand to leave with the first group.

I was toast. I was in an impossible position. I would have to quit and forfeit the severance package. I worked hard to reconcile myself to that. Neither of the other two of the original three asked to stay. I decided if that was what it took, I would pursue the new ministry. Then my supervisor's boss called me to his office.

"Don, I cleared it with my boss. You are still getting the severance," he said.

I went back to my station. Jack asked, "What did he say?"

I looked over to him. "I am going too . . . with the package." I realized I was not the only one relieved. The word spread through the department.

"I want you to know," Amanda, my shift leader, began during lunch, "We were all prepared to go into Ron's office and tell him he was letting you go too. You prepared to leave and had a place to go. It wasn't going to be fair to you." I saw a few of my coworkers nod affirmingly.

"Thank you," was all I could say. My father has often told me the sun shines on me. I almost never believe it, but that time I did.

I clocked out and turned in my keys on the last day. A coworker with a camcorder followed me outside with the others. She wanted to document the last group she would work with before she retired. One of the guys watching said, "She hated you when you got here three years ago."

"She wasn't the only one," I said.

"That's true. I can't believe what a change it is from then. The whole team is sorry you're leaving."

"Maybe I won," I said. I left putting bi-vocational ministry behind me. When I was bored and drinking, I often wished to have that job back. I wanted to be so covered up with work that I could beg off from dealing

---

1. North American Free Trade Agreement.

with the pettiness of some church people. On the other hand, the church would be an escape from the pressures of the secular job. Looking back, it felt like it had been a perfect situation. It was not. Nostalgic thoughts play tricks on us.

The danger of such nostalgia is that we ignore the present situation. The same holds true for desiring the future. We lose sight of what we have before us and could be turning to something better. It can be said that older folks escape by looking backward while younger people look to the future. Each group is exasperated with the other for not being in the present. It is a curious problem.

Being bi-vocational was when I thought I was doing nothing right or giving anything the proper attention. At the end of that time, I had a delightful precocious toddler and a newborn. My wife was trying to be supportive. I was not going to breathe too freely for too long. I was going to be a full-time student after five years and serve three small congregations. I was wondering if I would lose sunshine.

I needed the sun shining on me if I was going to find any open doors to my work. The first was at Green Meadow church. The congregation had been supportive of my work toward my doctorate. There was even a reception after I graduated. A couple from the church took Kathryn and me out to celebrate. I wondered what I could do there.

My second open door was at my local recovery group. I was encouraged to take part in as many meetings as I wanted to. I was also encouraged to do service work for my group. I attended book studies. I listened to insights old timers had. Someone said to me I should keep this thought in mind, "The times to go to a meeting are when you want to go, when you don't want to go, and when they are holding one." I have never done all three. But meetings and service work get me out of my head for a while.

I have one major character defect. I desire recognition for my good actions. I despise the desire. It makes very little sense to me that I should want it. It is outside of my ethical system. What is the point of doing good if you only want credit for doing it? And yet, I wanted to achieve something important. I wanted to be the hero. I am like the title character of "Lord Jim." I am always tempted to take refuge in a life of daydreams. Perhaps, that is why the movie appeals to me. Lord Jim is the tragic figure who could be the hero if he faced up to his fear of death. My fear has been the fear of failing and facing the repercussions of failure.

I have been jealous of those who get the credit I wish I could have had. Often, I did not try what they did because of my fear of failing. Other times, I did not get the credit even though I worked as hard. And then there were times when circumstances kept me from doing the same things. There were always excuses. It is hard to be both ambitious and anonymous.

Conversely, I am embarrassed when I am recognized or thanked for my good actions. I often wonder if I really *deserve* it. For instance, I have received recognition for visiting the sick in the hospitals and the nursing homes. "Thank you for coming," I am almost always told. Or take the times after a funeral service where I am told, "Thank you so much." And then there is even the polite gratitude expressed for leading worship, providing a sermon, and keeping all of it within a reasonable time.

I feel somewhat guilty on each occasion because I want the encounters to end quickly. As I pointed out in my amends letters, I wanted to end all such encounters so I could go home and drink. But drinking was only part of it. People tell me I do very well in social situations. Some are surprised when they learn I suffer depression. Looking for open doors is made much harder because of a sincere desire to never want to walk through them.

A woman I dated once told me, "You are not fair to yourself." She was correct. I am not fair to myself. It is hard for me to feel rewarded and to enjoy the good things that have come my way. My mind invariably turns to the people I think need goodness and deserve it more than I do. I often hear the words of John the Baptist saying, "Whoever has two coats must share with anyone who has none."[2] In many ways, I serve to salve my own conscience.

St. Paul describes this conundrum very well in Romans. He writes that he suffers from a personal ethical failure. He covets. He breaks the last of the Ten Commandments. He does not steal. But he has an inordinate desire for material goods. When he reads that one law, "You shall not covet your neighbor's wife. Nor shall you desire your neighbor's house, or field, or male or female slave, or ox, or donkey, or anything that belongs to your neighbor,"[3] he claims sin comes to life in him and destroys him. How does a person get beyond such a problem?

The next chapter in the Romans offers the understanding that even though St. Paul struggles in this way, he is forgiven. I am glad he included that thought! The matter does not end there. St. Paul knows he still struggles.

2. Luke 3:11b.
3. Exodus 20:17.

Despite all the talk some teachers say about a second working of grace, I see that my problem mirrors St. Paul's. If he was not freed from sinning, then I take comfort knowing that I am not while still being forgiven.

Growth is still possible. If we have the order of when St. Paul's letters were written correct, he took most of his life to overcome his issue and to honestly say the following, "for I have learned to be content with whatever I have."[4]

My problem is also an inordinate desire for the intangible feeling of being praised. For me at least, it is the most dangerous desire I have. I often hated watching people point heavenward when they received an award for their service. Because of my own feelings of discontent, I thought such people were really being fake. For all I really know they may have been. It does not matter though. I know if I had done it, I would have been fake.

The question remains, "Then why serve if doing so brings regret?" Good question. The thought behind it is the same as the one I have heard people say about attending worship. "If your attitude is not right, you don't need to be there just going through the motions." I take issue with that idea.

Immanuel Kant, the great German philosopher, offers an interesting thought about ethical behavior. If people act in such a way as to bring about good for someone else because they like the feeling they receive from it, then their action is suspect because the action could change with that motivation. This is a longer explanation of my father's dictum, "if you are doing it to be thanked, you are doing it for the wrong reason." In other words, doing good for others because it is good is the truly ethical position. Many people believe this is the true meaning of the word compassion. I am not sure I accept that completely. I can see that this is a position that eventually wears a person out. People, while growing morally and spiritually, need to be encouraged to do good. They do not need to be made to feel guilty. The task is simply helping a person realize that there will not be a major loss to themselves if they use their time or resources for the good of other people.

People have differing motives for not helping a person. One person may not feel safe in a certain area. One person has a moral block concerning how to help another person. Another person may have had bad experience in doing something for others. Whatever the motive not to help is, it should not be discounted. The person's concern should not be readily dismissed. It may even be best to find another means that the person can

4. Philippians 4:11b.

contribute to whatever the effort is. Recognizing my own ethical flaws helps me tolerate other people's flaws.

The United Methodist Church faces major problems because too many people do not recognize their own motives. It has torn the fabric of the discipline of the denomination. And it has brought schism. The last major separation of Methodism in America was in 1844 over the issue of slavery. The group that became known as the Methodist Episcopal Church, South decided that a person could own another person and force the slave to do whatever the master desired was morally acceptable. It was not until 1939 that the rift was healed. Even then regional jurisdictions were developed because of the mutual suspicions over who would have the most influence within the new denomination then called The Methodist Church. These regional conflicts threaten the unity of the church. Essentially, the unity only occurs when the General Conference of The United Methodist Church convenes every four years. The bishops gather more often, but there is no presiding bishop with any more authority than the others. It is a collegial gathering.

The difficulties for church unity are surpassed by the fact that when the denomination gets something right, it does a superb job of it just as my friend from my doctoral cohort said. The most popular agency for our church members is the United Methodist Committee on Relief or UMCOR.

"I don't like a lot of things our church does," one lay member told me during a meeting of the church council, "but I have no issue with UMCOR."

When the tragic Christmas Tsunami hit Sumatra and other islands in the South Pacific, I stood in the pulpit in one church, gave a brief description of the tragedy, and said, "There has been no directive or request given yet. I am sure UMCOR will be involved there and making requests from us. This week is a holiday break for most of us; and trying to coordinate putting an offering together will be difficult. With your permission, I would like to take a special offering designated for that relief so that when the request comes, we can quickly respond." The audience assented with enthusiastic applause.

I am proud of the work of that agency. I know of the work being done by others that I support. I have never opposed any work the General Boards have done that I learned about. It saddens me that these once open doors may be crippled by the denomination dividing. I am encouraged with a sincere belief that the good work of ministry will continue to be done.

The question causing the division is this. Is the denomination's stance on forbidding homosexual persons to be ordained and forbidding the practice of same sex wedding services consistent with our understanding of the faith from Jesus? While the official position has been that "homosexuality is incompatible with Christian teaching," it has not always been that way. The idea was adopted in 1972. The denomination's official statement on War is that it too is incompatible with Christian teaching. We do not forbid members of the denomination from serving in the armed forces or clergy from serving as military chaplains.

The issue that we euphemistically call human sexuality is part of the larger culture war that has overtaken the United States and Eastern Europe. There is a terrible work involved when the powers that be attempt to set church doctrines in ways to align the church with destructive political ideology.

The question about whether Christian tradition and the teachings of the Bible have any bearing on a modern discussion is valid. Using the teachings from both is valid. The Bible and Christian tradition are the lenses we use to interpret the world around us. There can be no Christian position on any moral matter without some sort of principle drawn from the Bible and Tradition. It is important to note too that human reason and human experience are involved in learning those principles. This Wesleyan quadrilateral is the intellectual framework we use in discussing issues among ourselves.

I learned this way from first standing outside of it. I understand the position of the adult convert who has looked closely at their own beliefs and analyzed another set of beliefs and chose the latter views. Internally, that person experienced a revolution of sorts. They have a new way of thinking, praying, and being. I also understand the experience of those cradle Methodists who never fully appreciated their position because it appeared in every way to them to be normal.

I am often frustrated by my brothers and sisters among the clergy who take the opposing side. Female clergy members who prefer the position that the church has taken up to this point fascinate me. Many evangelicals believe the Bible and tradition are relatively clear regarding the leadership of women in the churches. Yet, the denomination permits female clergy, including bishops. There is a justice concern involved. Women will continue to be considered second-class members and mistreated until female leaders are visible among us. The church decided that the principles of justice and equality before God had to be demonstrated in concrete ways. Simply saying a person is of sacred worth is not enough. One would think female clergy would understand the struggle for justice and equality before God for homosexual persons. Culture war is the only reason I can think of that would allow a person to compartmentalize their thinking in this way. It is a case of being able to see but choosing not to look.

The issue will be settled soon. We could see most lay people going one way while the majority of clergy go another. It will hasten the closing of many smaller churches.

Will there be open doors for doing ministry or will the clergy hear calls to develop new congregations and outreach in bi-vocational ministry? Or will the churches die and something else replace them? There will continue to be spiritual seekers. The question for them will be where can we go?

I honestly believe these concerns are what drives the momentum for a denominational division. Christianity is dying in the West. There may be other areas in the world where the faith is growing. I think the numbers that are reported are not very firm. The fact is I never hear or see any numbers that can be substantiated.

Lovett Weems called what is happening to The United Methodist Church in the United States a "death tsunami." He argues there will be a massive dying-off of the majority of our lay members in the next fifteen years. The anecdotal evidence shows this. If a children's ministry of thirty-five students like Wonderful Wednesday can constitute my "third church," then that demonstrates the relative sizes of the congregations I was serving at the time. The memories held by older church members do not help matters. They recall a time when their buildings were full of people, there were more children, and everyone had a good time together. I recall a time not so long ago when the average age of the lay members was fifty-five. Now it is more like seventy-five. Personally, I see little improvement.

The myth was perpetuated at the called General Conference in February 2019. On the final day of the debate on human sexuality, an African delegate claimed, "the church in Africa is growing by leaps and bounds because we hold to the teaching of the scriptures." It is a common myth. "If we just get back to the Bible," is a phrase that exposes the anxiety of the spiritually dead church. It describes the spiritual death that precedes the physical death of a church. A young woman who described herself as an evangelical from Texas made a similar claim. She claimed that not all young people supported a change in the church discipline because . . . get this . . . she was a young person. She characterized the self-focused understanding of Christian teaching that has caused many other young people to distrust the evangelical movement.

The time I have spent learning bad behavior and then unlearning it demonstrates to me the difficulty of the church overcoming these problems. Bad morals, behaviors, and prejudice plague the communities the churches reside among. I wonder if the change in myself was not easier than anything that may be reasonably expected in the church culture.

The solution that many clergy and lay people wish to try is merely a reflection of the problem of the secular communities. There can be no sense of self-reflection because it may expose one's real motives. An inner voice becomes louder so that the sense of immediacy and crisis stops any suggestion that we may be on the wrong path. This demonic inner voice has appeared in so many people at one time that we cannot do anything except continue running along the broad way that leads to destruction.

I remember the words of the instructor when I was learning water safety. If it is possible to extend a tool (a rope, a life preserver, a pole, or a tree branch) to a drowning person, do it. The last resort to save another person was to get into the water with them. The drowning person is panicking, fearing for their life. It does not matter if that person is your best friend, sibling, father, or mother. The drowning person will do anything to stay alive. They will try to get on top of you, and in the process, they will drown you and themselves. This is the situation of Christianity in America in general and my denomination in particular. We are drowning and trying to save ourselves by standing on each other. The attitude should change, and the panic struggle be stopped. We have a voice on the shore telling us to grab hold of something better. We refuse to listen.

Chapter 11

When Life Is Sick

I understand why people want to give up on living. I live in an area of the United States where country music is popular. Country music is fatalist if it is anything. Life is what it is. Life is loss. A joke we told during the time when the idiotic conspiracy theory of backward masking was in vogue among fundamentalists was, "What do you get when you play country music records backwards?" The answer/punchline was, "You get your wife back, your dog back, and your pickup truck back."

Many rural, working-class people understand life is difficult and sometimes harsh. The attitude that keeps one alive is an almost Victorian understanding of virtuous labor. If we work hard, we can keep the evils of poverty away from us. When a neighbor was considered unworthy, it was because the doctrine of virtuous labor was violated.

I once performed a social media experiment where I demonstrated this doctrine at work. I posted on Facebook an observation that the two texts from the letters of Paul said, "Thieves must give up stealing: rather let them labor and work honestly with their own hands, so as to have something to share with the needy,"[1] and, "For even when we were with you, we gave you this command: Anyone unwilling to work should not eat."[2] I wanted to see what people made from these texts being set side by side. The results should not have been surprising.

1. Ephesians 4:28.
2. 2 Thessalonians 3:10.

The post generated many "likes." One parishioner shared it and congratulated me on my wisdom. Other comments showed me something I was not expecting. Most people read the two texts together as saying, "Thieves should not eat." It was not the point I was making. In fact, I was trying to get people to see that the texts were to be held together in tension.

A parishioner in a church I had served earlier in my career told me one day, "Nothing in the Bible says I have to give anyone anything I earn from my work." I thought of several examples and decided on the text from Ephesians I quoted above. He looked at me a moment. "Well, it does not say how much I should give," he concluded. I nodded affirmatively while sighing deeply in my soul.

The Ephesians text says nothing about laboring for one's food, clothing, and shelter. It says nothing about luxuries. What it says is that takers can become givers. And that if someone is in need through no fault of their own, then they deserve to eat. The Thessalonians text argues against idlers who would not be in need except for the fact that they are busy with nonsense.

The goal of both texts is to preserve and enhance the dignity of people we call sinners—in these cases thieves and busybodies. Those people in need also deserve to have their dignity respected and possibly enhanced. This is the very reason I argue that ministry is meant to be mutual. A thief that does not know a way to make a living requires guidance on how to do it. A busybody should be told the equivalent of, "Get in here and set the table if you want any supper." Why? Because grace instructs. The Jewish people regard the Books of Moses not as much as the "Law of Moses" but the instruction of Moses. The grace taught by the Scriptures is one that brings dignity to the human condition. The opposite of grace is not work. It is condemnation.

Condemnation makes life sick. It is simply a problem of inducing guilt into another person. When I hear a person mourning the thought that their sins caused the death of Jesus, I cringe. The flipside is the idea that is expressed this way, "If I had been the only person in need of a savior, Jesus would have still died for me." It is egotism with an inferiority complex. It is how an addict thinks about his or her own life. It is sick.

There is nothing inherently wrong with failing. The only possible failure that is detrimental is the kind that ends someone's life. Even then, the effort put in to save one's own life or someone else's, is regarded as heroic yet tragic. It is when every failure is treated as a life-and-death issue. Failure to get good grades, to arrive at an appointment on time, to miss a meeting, to file the proper paperwork on time, and a host of other failures really do not matter. When these failures are put on a par with the life-and-death issue, it brings condemnation—including self-condemnation—which brings with it guilt.

My biggest problem was both viewing myself as the center of everything and the center of everything that ever went wrong. I wanted nothing more than to be a hero of some sort. I could be proven right about everything. I could be center stage. I could make requests that would always be honored. And, at the same time, I believed I could never do any of that. I also never could develop the talent to do anything that would bring me those accolades I desired.

I often found over time that I could never get congregations to accept some actions that they did not want to take. If I could show that costs and income could not sustain actions, if I could show that actions did not change costs and income, or if I showed that certain actions were detrimental to the well-being of the church, I was never believed by enough people to stave off the calamity. The times I did prove the point and motivated enough people to do something about it, I found that I was often condemned for it. I was not the hero. I was the bad guy. Why was that? It appeared to be the catch-22. Whatever I did, it did not seem to work, and the failure brought condemnation, which brought about resentments in myself.

Life became increasingly insane. I did not understand that it was my part that caused the insanity to grow. I resented that I maintained a job and a roof over the heads of my family, while going to school. My father often said he was amazed by my accomplishment, but my resentment increased simply because I assumed my wife treated it as her due. The resentment became worse when I included babysitting and school drop-off and pick-up to my list of jobs while my wife went to school without having any other responsibility save for household help.

It all went back to my desire to be the hero, the savior, or the superman. She was not the first person I became involved with who was going to be that way either. Many young women I dated before her were the same way. I was trying to be a hero. I thought that they needed me to make their lives better. There was a secret about to be revealed to me. I cannot make anyone's life better.

I can only make my own life better. Trying to help someone else overhaul their life was always going to be disastrous, and such disasters were not supposed to happen, or so I thought. Yet, there were any number of signs that disasters would always occur.

One example of such a sign was in my tendency to argue until I convinced the other person. I do not know why I believed that could ever work. It never would work on me, after all. I once remarked after reading David McCollough's biography of President John Adams that his greatest personal failing was his intention to say in effect, I am right. I know I am right. And we are going to sit here and discuss it until you know it, too.

A woman I taught in a Sunday night class would tell me after an evening session that once in awhile, I should let someone else be right. I had a high opinion of my opinion. I would belabor the point when someone disagreed with me. It was arrogant and presumptive. It was also what many teachers had patterned to me as a student. It never occurred to me that those same teachers were often the authors of their own misery. I followed the pattern to the end. I needed to make some major changes.

I decided to continue with what I was doing. I could see recalcitrance in other people, even whole groups of people. I knew I could be the same way, but I thought I was justified in being so. My new mantra with other people was, "I give you every right to be wrong."

Jesus cautioned his listeners to first remove the beam from our own eye before we could remove the splinter from someone else's.[3] It is an oft-quoted passage. The ones who quote it forget that in the previous chapter there is this warning. "The eye is the lamp of the body. So, if your eye is healthy your whole body will be full of light; but if your eye is unhealthy, your whole body will be filled with darkness. If then the light in you is darkness, how great is the darkness?"[4] It sounds very "commonsensical." Light must get into the eye so a person can see. If not, the person is blind. So far so good. But the writer asks what happens when the light itself is darkness?

We may find it easy to assume that the question is a twist of rhetoric that makes the idea of blindness stronger. The light that enters the eye being dark is the failure of seeing something as it is. Just as we cannot clearly see the splinter in someone else's eye unless we remove the obstacle that blocks our own vision, we may not know our vision is blocked because we refuse to see life as it is. We may not be able to recognize our own sickness.

I knew my life was sick. I thought it was sick because of everyone else in it. The other people in my life were sick too. I contributed to their

---

3. See Matthew 7:3.
4. Matthew 6:20–22.

sickness just as they contributed to mine. None of us really could see how our own vision was being distorted by our own self-diagnoses.

My attempts to self-medicate only made matters worse. It was detrimental to both my physical and mental health. My son was correct when he told me I was not the person I used to be before my drinking took hold. I thought he was mistaken. He verbalized this thought the best way he could. He is not at fault for not explaining it better. I asked his mother later that day her thoughts about it. She agreed. I believed they had discussed the issue previously. The heroes in many stories have people who refuse to listen to them. I was of course the hero of my own story. I was not wrong because of this. I was wrong because there was something wrong with my viewpoint. I could not understand that. All people are complicated. And all people complicate things.

When life is sick it is difficult to find the cure. A truly sick person may know where the pain is but not know why it hurts. Good physical health care is essential. Good mental health care is just as crucial because physical illness and mental illness often go together. Good spiritual health is essential too. One can deal with the other two problems and continue to be miserable. Worse yet, the unspiritual person causes spiritual misery in other people.

There is a question asked by evangelism instructors. "What is both better than going to heaven and worse than going to hell?" The answer is, "Taking someone with you." Granted the theology behind the question and answer is atrocious. Like many bad ideas that catch on, it holds a kernel of truth within it. Making other people miserable does not help you in the least. The misery that you spread makes your own worse. I have both seen enough of it and done enough of it to know it is true.

The great spiritual masters and saints do not attempt to make other people happy. These people practice contentment and happiness by being content and happy. They do so by a variety of spiritual means. Prayer, meditation, reading, walking, sitting still, listening, praising, working, eating, and drinking can all be spiritual practices when a person lives by one or more spiritual principles. Spiritual disciplines are meant to *teach* oneself.

St. Paul's letter to the Philippians uses the words "joy" and "rejoice" seven times in four chapters. As I quoted in the previous chapter, Paul claims contentment and joy after years of struggling with his own moral failure. He makes no claim in the letter that his happiness is contingent on the actions of other people. He does urge two people to be reconciled and in their reconciliation they may be content. He calls on them to stop spreading their mutual misery. Whether they do or not has no bearing on his own happiness. Most of the clergy members I know would like to have this contentment.

Clergy believe that the success or the failure of the congregation depends on their work. It does not. But the fact never matters to the lay leaders of the church. Clergy take a lot of externalized angst. Pastors often become symptom bearers for the congregations. The leadership of bishops and superintendents fails to help the situation. There is little they can do. It is tragic. How does a person live with it?

Recognizing the sickness for what it is helps one live with it. Know that it is an illness of the spirit that is not yours to take on for the other people.

The sickness should go back to where it belongs. Other people may want the clergy to share the sickness another person demonstrates. It may be that it infects a group of people, but it does not belong to the pastor. It cannot be cured by the pastor. I have decided not to try any longer.

The happiness and contentment of the saints attracted other people to them to learn their own contentment. We can look for others who have that and find out how to do what they do to find it. I believe ultimately that is why the great spiritual works were written. The people who lived their lives by spiritual principles and disciplines either wrote or were written about so that some people may find ways out of unhappiness.

Helping other people find their way out of addiction and other forms of misery is one reason this confession has been written. The main reason is to see where the distortion in my own vision exists. In that regard it has been eye opening. I see that many of the faults I saw in others over the years were mine too. I see how difficult I was to be around before and after walking my road to recovery and life started. I also see how hard it has been for others around me to be around me.

Life is better. I am building a new life with Kathryn. She tells me her grandfather nicknamed her Sunshine. My ministry is being restored. I continue working on rebuilding my relationship with my sons. I am on the cusp of forging new relationships with Kathryn's sons. A new congregation awaits my leadership.

The denomination is splintering. Like watching a loved one slowly die, it will be a relief when it is done. Yet, it will nevertheless be tragic. Like life, I will approach this issue one day at a time while practicing my spiritual disciplines and finding if I can some contentment within the trouble.

I am ending this memoir at the beginning of the COVID-19 pandemic. Like everyone else I am both concerned and frustrated. I am not angry. I am not afraid. I do not wish to lose any family or friends or neighbors. There have been a lot of losses for many other people. I see no reason to think I should be exempt. As with the denominational division, I will greet each day with spiritual practice and do what I can to remain healthy.

Afterword

THE PHONE IN THE church office rang. I answered. Instead of the common robocall from a group claiming to be a ministry or ministries, this was a person offering free services to the church.

"We are a local recovery program for men," the gentleman began. "In trying to help our guys in their recovery from drugs and alcohol, we send them out to do small construction or landscaping jobs for churches. If you are happy with the results, we only ask the church to make a donation to our ministry."

"How long is your program?" I asked.

"Anywhere between twelve and sixteen months," was the reply.

"Sixteen months? Why so long?"

"In recovery, it takes a lot of service work."

When the conversation ended, I was left wondering if I was hearing from something akin to the chickenplant recovery described in chapter six. I went over to one of the other offices and asked if anyone had heard of the program.

"Oh, yes," one lady replied, "they did some really good work at my sister's church." Another person told me something similar.

I did not ask the ministry if they were a twelve-step program, but I asked about their certification. They claimed to hold licenses from the state of Tennessee as both an IOP clinic and a halfway house. The claim appears to be legitimate.

I know one person who went through their program. He gave it a glowing testimonial. However, the judge was not impressed and sentenced the man to prison.

Reflecting on my own recovery and continuing research into the ideas behind it, I have begun asking how much recovery programs have become cultish. Amanda Montell in her book *Cultish: The Language of Fanaticism* uses Alcoholics Anonymous as an example of a group that is cult-like in their language while not being a cult. In fact, she supports what AA is trying to do to help people. My question is how do groups using twelve-step and other recovery language become cults?

Sixteen months of "service work" that leads to fundraising sounds extreme to me. I certainly would have balked at such a requirement. It reminds me of the movie "Holes" where Shia LaBeouf's character, Stanley Yelnats, is told that digging holes will turn a bad boy into a good boy only to learn the digging is a search for buried treasure.

Recovery programs or ministries should not add to the stigma of addiction. Attempts to control the behavior of addicted people never help them. In the same way, deciding that recovering addicts or alcoholics are only useful for helping others in recovery continues the stigma and ultimately makes recovering harder. Recovering addicts are not in any way more or less human than we once were. Never paint pictures of hopelessness to better tell stories of miracles.

Appendix A

THIS IS THE FIRST step questionnaire that was used in 2018 at Cornerstone of Recovery. The errors in spelling and punctuation are in the original.

POWERLESSNESS

1. What does Powerlessness mean to you?

2. How have you previously tried to control your use of alcohol and/or other drugs?

    a. When? Think back to your earliest attempts to control.

    b. What did you do to control?

    c. Reasons for attempts to control

    d. Lengths of periods of abstinence.

    e. Reasons you gave yourself for resumption of use.

3. Alcohol and/or other drug usage.

    a. Kinds

    b. Amounts

    c. Frequency—includes time of day, weekends only, binge drinking, etc.

4. Loss of memory and blackouts while intoxicated. Recall situations where your memory loss was brought to your attention, especially if

you were accused of unacceptable behavior. Recall times you had no recollection of prior events.

5. Preoccupation—reflect on how your thinking revolved around use of alcohol and/or other drugs. This includes planning the day around drug use or thinking about times when you will be free to drink or take drugs.

6. Discuss activities you have engaged in to obtain alcohol or other drugs when not available or you lacked money. This could include theft of money from spouse, children, friends, employers, or others. Drinking shaving lotion or other unusual beverages containing alcohol; selling off household or personal items for money, etc. (sic)

7. Legal Problems—include DWI charges, and other arrests directly related to alcohol or drug use, e.g. fighting, arrests for public intoxication, etc.

UNMANAGEABILITY

1. What is your definition of unmanageability?

2. Physical or mental condition. (Note: Lack of physical problems does not preclude possibility of alcohol/drug dependency).

3. Social Life: What is your social life like? Do you associate with people who drink like you do? Do you avoid non-drinking people and situations? Do you find yourself avoiding social contacts entirely?

4. Family Life: Indicate impact drinking has made on family relationships

    a. Spouse

    b. Children

    c. In-laws

    d. Parents

    e. Brothers/Sisters

    f. Other relatives

5. Economics: What impact has your drinking had upon your present economic condition? How much does your drinking or other drug

use cost per day, week, month, year (include nondrug purchases, e.g DWI fines, legal costs, etc.)? What economic prices have you and your family had to pay as a result of channeling money into drinking and drug use? Think of times when alcohol/drugs purchased took precedence over domestic needs.

6. Occupation: Indicate impact alcohol/drugs have had on employment.

    a. Promotions

    b. Are you where you feel you should be salary wise?

    c. How many alcohol or other drug related job changes have you had? Discuss.

    d. Have you ever been discharged from a position? Reason for discharge may not have been given as alcohol and drug use—but you know—think back.

    e. Is your present job in jeopardy? Does your employer know you are in treatment?

    f. Absenteeism: What is the frequency and pattern of your absenteeism? Do you call in sick on Mondays because you are hung over from the weekend?

7. Spiritual Life: Has there been deterioration in your spiritual life? Do you have vague spiritual desires?

8. Emotional or feeling: Give five examples of feelings and emotions you have tried to alter with the use of alcohol or other drugs? Example: Guilt.

Please write down what you have determined working the First Step.

If after reviewing the First Step you feel you need help. Please give at least five reasons why you should continue on with treatment.

Bibliography

Adams, Patch. *House Calls: How We Can All Heal the World One Visit at a Time.* San Francisco: Robert D. Reed, 1998.

Anonymous. *Alcoholics Anonymous.* New York: Alcoholics Anonymous World Services, Inc., 2001.

Anonymous. *Narcotics Anonymous.* Chatsworth, CA: Narcotics Anonymous World Service, 2008.

Dodes, Lance, and Zachary Dodes. *The Sober Truth: Debunking the Bad Science Behind 12-Step Programs and the Rehab Industry.* Boston: Beacon, 2014.

Harris, Amy Julia, and Soshana Walter. "They Thought They Were Going to Rehab. They Ended Up in Chicken Plants." *Reveal: From the Center for Investigative Reporting,* October 4, 2017.

Montell, Amanda. *Cultish: The Language of Fanaticism.* New York. HarperCollins, 2021.

Trimpey, Jack. *Rational Recovery.* New York: Pocket, 1996.

Young, Jeffrey E., and Janet S. Klosko. *Reinventing Your Life: The Breakthrough Program to End Negative Behavior . . . and Feel Great Again.* New York: Plume, 1994.